THE MAGICAL
WORLDS OF
HARRY POTTER

THE MAGICAL WORLDS OF HARRY POTTER

A Treasury of Myths,
Legends and Fascinating Facts

DAVID COLBERT

PUFFIN

PUFFIN BOOKS

Published by the Penguin Group
Penguin Books Ltd, 80 Strand, London WC2R 0RL, England
Penguin Putnam Inc., 375 Hudson Street, New York, New York 10014, USA
Penguin Books Australia Ltd, 250 Camberwell Road, Camberwell, Victoria 3124,
Australia
Penguin Books Canada Ltd, 10 Alcorn Avenue, Toronto, Ontario, Canada M4V 3B2
Penguin Books India (P) Ltd, 11 Community Centre, Panchsheel Park,
New Delhi – 110 017, India
Penguin Books (NZ) Ltd, Cnr Rosedale and Airborne Roads, Albany, Auckland,
New Zealand
Penguin Books (South Africa) (Pty) Ltd, 24 Sturdee Avenue, Rosebank 2196, South
Africa

Penguin Books Ltd, Registered Offices: 80 Strand, London WC2R 0RL, England

www.penguin.com

First published 2001
First published in this edition 2003
8

Set in Adobe Garamond

Made and printed in England by Clays Ltd, St Ives plc

British Library Cataloguing in Publication Data
A CIP catalogue record for this book is available from the British Library

ISBN 0–141–31738–8

For my nieces Emma, Lillian, and Molly, and my nephew Sam

Read myths with the eyes of wonder:
the myths transparent to their universal meaning,
their meaning transparent to its mysterious source.

The first of Joseph Campbell's
Ten Commandments for Reading Mythology

Contents

Guide to abbreviations of the book titles:

Harry Potter and the Philosopher's Stone: Stone

Harry Potter and the Chamber of Secrets: Chamber

Harry Potter and the Prisoner of Azkaban: Azkaban

Harry Potter and the Goblet of Fire: Goblet

Harry Potter and the Order of the Phoenix: Phoenix

Fantastic Beasts and Where to Find Them: Beasts

Quidditch Through the Ages: Quidditch

The *Harry Potter* books by J. K. Rowling are published by Bloomsbury Publishing PLC

NOTE FOR THE SECOND EDITION: If you're a returning reader you'll discover that several new chapters were added and many others were updated after the publication of *Harry Potter and the Order of the Phoenix*. You'll find a surprising source for the Order of the Phoenix; the legends behind the Death Eaters; an extensive chapter on the potions brewed by Professor Snape; a hard look at Inquisitor Dolores Umbridge; unexpected insights into Herbology; the stories behind Rowling's most interesting names yet; and dozens of new sidebars with fun facts. I hope you enjoy it. – D.C.

Introduction

ONE OF THE PLEASURES OF READING J. K. ROWLING IS discovering the playful references to history, legend and literature that she hides in her books. For instance, the Sphinx in the maze during the Triwizard Tournament asks a riddle, just as the Sphinx of ancient Greek mythology did. Hagrid's pet dog, Fluffy, is actually another famous beast from Greek mythology, Cerberus. 'Durmstrang', the name of the wizarding school that admits only full-blooded wizards and has questionable links to Lord Voldemort, comes from a German artistic style called *Sturm und Drang*, which was a favourite of Nazi Germany. As well, Durmstrang students arrive at Hogwarts in a ship like the one featured prominently in a famous *Sturm und Drang* opera. Alert readers know Rowling also hides fun clues in the names she chooses for characters. Draco, Harry's nemesis, gets his name from the Latin word for 'dragon' or 'snake'. Dumbledore's pet phoenix, Fawkes, gets his name from a historical figure linked to bonfires just as phoenixes are said to be reborn in fire.

This book decodes her clues to reveal the artfully hidden

meanings. In an online chat with fans, she encouraged one reader who asked the origin of a particular phrase to go and look it up. Rowling clearly believes that her readers should do some investigating of their own. That's what *The Magical Worlds of Harry Potter* is about: a little investigation, in a spirit of fun. The point is to entertain, amuse, and fascinate.

You may even be sharing a laugh with Rowling herself. As *TIME* magazine said when noting that Hogwarts caretaker Argus Filch gets his name from the Argus of Greek mythology, a watchman with a thousand eyes on his body, 'it's the sort of touch that can prompt an author's inward smile.'

If you've never noticed those clues, don't feel alone. One of Rowling's amazing gifts is her ability to toss them out without breaking stride in telling her story. For example, she's happy to make only a passing reference in *Harry Potter and the Prisoner of Azkaban* to a manticore – a nasty, man-eating, imaginary beast. Skipping the opportunity to describe that creature in detail takes discipline. But for Rowling, it's just a casual reference. Still, when you know what a manticore is, and that it has appeared in legends for thousands of years, Rowling's story is all the more satisfying.

J. R. R. Tolkien, author of *The Hobbit* and *The Lord of the Rings*, refers to a 'cauldron' of ideas to describe an ever-cooking pot of ideas, themes and characters from which every writer takes, and to which every writer adds. Though the fictional world created by J. K. Rowling is unique, it grows from a deep foundation of myths and folklore that have endured across distance and time. The popularity of Rowling's books testifies to the breadth of culture from which she draws many of her images, characters, and themes. This book reveals that broader realm to fans whose awareness has been awakened by reading Rowling. As you'll see, she creates something entirely new with the bits of material from which she draws; yet she remains remarkably true to the essence of each.

Did Alchemists Really Search for a Magic Stone?

JUST WHAT WERE ALCHEMISTS TRYING TO do? Did they accomplish anything, or did all their work disappear in a cloud of smoke?

Anyone who has read *Stone* knows that alchemy is an ancient mix of chemistry and magic. Alchemists tried to create gold from less valuable metals, and to concoct a potion that could cure all ills and make the drinker immortal.

The ancient Arab world is credited with the development of alchemy. The name comes from the Arab term *al-kimia* ('the transformation of metals'), which also gives us the word 'chemistry'. Alchemy's origins go back even further. The Arab term was borrowed from ancient Greek, and seems to have first appeared in Egypt. There is also evidence of alchemy in ancient China and India.

'The Stone will do it. She shall feel gold, taste gold, hear gold, sleep gold . . .'

Ben Jonson
The Alchemist
(1610)
(Act IV, scene I)

We tend to think of alchemists as greedy and overreaching, obsessed with wealth and immortality. But some people say their work laid the foundation for modern chemistry. Indeed, real scientists studied alchemy. Sir Isaac Newton, the physicist and mathematician, wrote millions of words on the subject. However, in keeping with tradition, Newton was secretive about his alchemy experiments – at one point urging another alchemist to keep 'high silence' about the work.

Just as the Arabic word *al-kimia* gives us the terms 'alchemy' and 'chemistry', Arabic mathematics, once the most advanced in the world, offers another term we hear in classroom today: *al-gebr*. It means 'equalize', which is what students do with the two sides of an equation in algebra.

The Metropolis of Alchemy

During the late 1500s two emperors hired the world's leading alchemists to work in the city of Prague in what is now the Czech Republic. This led to a nickname for the city: 'the Metropolis of Alchemy'. Emperors, however, can be fickle. When a British alchemist, Edward Kelley, failed to create gold, he was thrown in a dungeon. Even the efforts of Britain's Queen Elizabeth I failed to win his release. He died trying to escape.

Of course, there were many frauds. A story is told of the arrival in Prague during that era of a stranger from Arabia, who invited the city's wealthiest men to a banquet where he promised to multiply the gold they brought. After gathering the offerings he prepared a mixture of chemicals and odd ingredients, such as eggshells and horse manure. This blend proved to be a stinkbomb, which permitted the charlatan a quick escape with the gold.

The Philosopher's Stone

One source calls the actual process followed by alchemists 'hopelessly complicated'. However, the basics were simple. According to the standard theory, all metals were a combination of mercury and sulphur. The more yellow the

The original title of the first adventure, *Harry Potter and the Philosopher's Stone*, appeared on books in the United Kingdom, Canada, Australia, and other territories. It was changed to *Harry Potter and the Sorcerer's Stone* by the American publisher, because 'Sorcerer's' seemed more exciting.

metal, the more sulphur in the mixture. So combining sulphur with mercury, in the right proportion and with the proper sequence of steps, would create gold.

Eventually, alchemists became frustrated with simple methods that did not work. They began to search for a magic ingredient, which they called the philosopher's stone. Some alchemists continued to believe the magic ingredient was simply sulphur. However, in *Harry Potter and the Philosopher's Stone* it is described as 'blood-red,' so Rowling probably had one of the more interesting formulas in mind.

See also:
Flamel
Fluffy
Mirrors

Who Was the Most Amazing Animagus?

ADDING *MAGUS*, THE LATIN WORD FOR 'wizard', to *animal*, J. K. Rowling coined the term 'Animagus': a wizard who can become an animal yet retain magical powers.

The ability to transform into an animal is as old as legend. In Celtic mythology, transformation into stags, boars, swans, eagles and ravens is common. Shamans in Native American cultures often transform into animals, usually birds.

One of the first wizards to display this ability was Proteus, of Greek mythology. He was a servant of Poseidon, god of the oceans. Proteus enjoyed a special talent: the knowledge of past, present and future. Unfortunately, this meant he was often being asked for predictions. To get away from people he would quickly transform into a variety of animals and terrifying creatures. Something that changes shape is still said to be 'protean'. This

Eagle-man totem figure from the Haida of the Pacific Northwest.

23

is the source of the Protean Charm in *Phoenix*, which Hermione puts on galleons carried by members of Dumbledore's Army. It makes the coins' serial numbers change to tell members when to meet. In keeping with the high status of Proteus in mythology, the Proteus Charm is advanced magic, not something even a fifth-year Hogwarts student would normally know. The other students are impressed.

Some of
J. K. Rowling's
Animagi:

**Minerva
McGonagall**
can be a cat.

James Potter
became a stag,
leading to his
nickname,
'Prongs'.

**Peter
Pettigrew**,
'Wormtail',
disguised
himself as
Ron's pet rat,
Scabbers.

DUELLING ANIMAGI

This sort of rapid-fire shape-shifting was remembered by the author T. H. White, whose novel *The Sword in the Stone* retells the legend of young King Arthur and his tutor, Merlin (spelled 'Merlyn' by White). Merlin battles another sorcerer, Madame Mim, in one of the most imaginative duels in literature:

> The object of the wizard in the duel was to turn himself into some kind of animal, vegetable or mineral which would destroy

the particular animal, vegetable or mineral that had been selected by his opponent. Sometimes it went on for hours . . .

At the first gong Madame Mim immediately turned herself into a dragon. It was the accepted opening move and Merlyn ought to have replied by being a thunderstorm or something like that. Instead, he caused a great deal of preliminary confusion by becoming a field mouse, which was quite invisible in the grass, and nibbled Madame Mim's tail, as she stared about in all directions, for about five minutes before she noticed him. But when she did notice the nibbling, she was a furious cat in two flicks.

Wart [Arthur] held his breath to see what the mouse would become next – he thought perhaps a tiger that could kill the cat – but Merlyn merely became another cat. He stood opposite her and made faces. This most irregular procedure put Madame Mim quite out of her stride, and it took her more than a minute to regain her bearings and become a dog. Even as she became it, Merlyn was another dog standing opposite her, of the same sort.

Some Animagi (cont.)

Sirius Black, whose name means 'black dog', can be one.

Rita Skeeter can become a beetle.

'Oh, well played, sir!' cried the Wart, beginning to see the plan.

Madame Mim was furious ... She had better alter her own tactics and give Merlyn a surprise ...

T. H. White's Merlyn also changed Arthur into animals, to teach him each animal's skills.

She had decided to try a new tack by leaving the offensive to Merlyn, beginning by assuming a defensive shape herself. She turned into a spreading oak.

Merlyn stood baffled under the oak for a few seconds. Then he most cheekily – and, as it turned out, rashly – became a powdery little blue-tit, which flew up and sat perkily on Madame Mim's branches. You could see the oak boiling

with indignation for a moment; but then its rage became icy cold, and the poor little blue-tit was sitting, not on an oak, but on a snake. The snake's mouth was open, and the bird was actually perching on its jaws. As the jaws clashed together, but only in the nick of time, the bird whizzed off as a gnat into the safe air. Madame Mim had got it on the run, however, and the speed of the contest now became bewildering. The quicker the attacker could assume a form, the less time the fugitive had to think of a form that would elude it, and now the changes were as quick as thought.

The battle ends when Madame Mim changes herself into an aullay, an animal that looks like an enormously large horse with the trunk of an elephant. She charges at Merlyn, but he simply disappears. Suddenly,

... strange things began to happen. The aullay got hiccoughs, turned red, swelled visibly, began whooping, came out in spots, staggered three times, rolled its eyes, fell rumbling to the ground. It groaned, kicked and said Farewell ...

The ingenious magician had turned

The duel in *The Sword in the Stone* was inspired by the Welsh legend of Cerridwen and Taliesen. (See page 53)

himself successively into the microbes, not yet discovered, of hiccoughs, scarlet fever, mumps, whooping cough, measles and heat spots, and from a complication of all these complaints the infamous Madame Mim had immediately expired.

ROWLING'S RULES

A great difference between Rowling's world and that of other authors is the restriction on Animagi. According to Rowling, this ability is highly regulated by the Ministry of Magic, which keeps track of wizards with this skill. In most other fictional worlds, wizards are capable of becoming any animal they please.

Perhaps Rowling is aware of the risks of taking animal form. In *Quidditch Through the Ages* she warns, 'The witch or wizard who finds him- or herself transfigured into a bat may take to the air, but, having a bat's brain, they are sure to forget where they want to go the moment they take flight.' Another famous writer, Ursula K. Le Guin, describes in a story titled *A Wizard of Earthsea* what can happen to wizards who aren't careful:

> As a boy, Ogion like all boys had thought it would be a very pleasant game to take

J. K. Rowling says one's personality is a factor in determining what animal one can become. She once said that she would like to transform herself into an otter, as it is her favourite animal. As we learn in *Phoenix*, that is the shape of **Hermione's Patronus**. No surprise there, because Rowling has said Hermione is a lot like her.

by art-magic whatever shape one liked, man or beast, tree or cloud, and so to play at a thousand beings. But as a wizard he had learned the price of the game, which is the peril of losing one's self, playing away the truth. The longer a man stays in a form not his own, the greater this peril. Every prentice-sorcerer learns the tale of the wizard Bordger of Way, who delighted in taking bear's shape, and did so more and more often until the bear grew in him and the man died away, and he became a bear, and killed his own little son in the forests, and was hunted down and slain. And no one knows how many of the dolphins that leap in the waters of the Inmost Sea were men once, wise men, who forgot their wisdom and their name in the joy of the restless sea.

Odin, the chief god of Norse mythology, is a sorcerer who often changes into animals. Zeus, the chief god of Greek mythology, does the same in many legends.

This is just the sort of risk that Harry, who often pushes himself beyond ordinary boundaries, might be expected to face. But J. K. Rowling says Harry will not become an Animagus as his father and godfather did. The training takes too much time, and he is too busy fighting Voldemort.

A Bug's Life

In *Phoenix*, Rowling introduces a new kind of shape-shifter, Nymphadora Tonks, who is a 'Metamorphmagus'. Rowling invented that word in the same way as 'Animagus'. She combined 'magus' with 'metamorphosis', which means the same in English as in ancient Greek: to change or transform.

Nymphadora's name refers to the same idea. At first glance, it may remind readers of nymphs, the young female nature spirits in Greek mythology. And just as Nymphadora Tonks's mother is named Andromeda, the Greek nymphs are linked to a mythological Andromeda. That character, a princess, was punished severely by the sea god, Poseidon, when her mother said she was as beautiful as the sea nymphs. However, there's more to the name Nymphadora. The original Greek word *nymph* referred to young brides who had just changed from one stage of life to another. Later it was used by scientists to describe insects going through the process of changing their shape.

See also:

Black, Sirius
McGonagall

Is 'Avada Kedavra' a Real Curse?

IN HARRY'S WORLD, THIS IS THE KILLING curse, the worst of the three Unforgivable Curses, any of which can bring a life term in Azkaban for a wizard who uses it against another human. It is the curse that Lord Voldemort used to kill Harry's parents, the one with which he tried to kill Harry, and, sadly, the fatal blow to Cedric Diggory. Harry is the only person known to survive it.

Although J. K. Rowling invents most of her spells and curses entirely from her imagination, the Avada Kedavra curse derives from a phrase in an ancient Middle Eastern language called Aramaic. *Abhadda kedhabhra* means 'disappear like this word'. It was used by ancient wizards to make illnesses disappear. However, there's no proof it was ever used to kill anyone.

The phrase is one likely origin of the magical word *abracadabra*. Now just part of a magician's entertaining chatter, that word was

A phoney legend says Egyptian King Tutankhamen's tomb was carved with this curse: 'Death will come on swift wings to whoever disturbs the pharaoh'. It was invented by a newspaper when one of the discoverers died soon after the tomb was opened.

once used by doctors. Quintus Serenus Sammonicus, a Roman physician who lived about AD 200, used it as a spell to make fever vanish. According to his prescription, it was to be written eleven times on a piece of paper, with one letter 'disappearing' each time:

In most cases, a **charm** is a bit of temporary magic that can be good or bad; a **jinx** will bring bad luck, but nothing serious; **curses** and **hexes** involve evil; and **spells** are serious magic that last a long time.

ABRACADABRA
ABRACADABR
ABRACADAB
ABRACADA
ABRACAD
ABRACA
ABRAC
ABRA
ABR
AB
A

The paper was to be tied around the patient's neck with flax for nine days, then tossed over the shoulder into a stream running to the east. When the water dissolved the words, the fever would disappear. The popularity of this cure grew in the centuries after Sammonicus, and it was even used to make the Black Death disappear. Clever readers will notice that this remedy, if it does nothing else, lets time pass. Because many diseases run their course naturally in a week or two, the spell probably did not do any good at all. On the other hand, it didn't hurt.

See also:
Latin

Are Basilisks Just Big Snakes?

BASILISKS ARE AMONG THE MOST DREADED magical creatures. 'Of the many fearsome beasts and monsters that roam our land,' Hermione reads in Rowling's *Harry Potter and the Chamber of Secrets*, 'there is none more curious or more deadly.'

The basilisk is certainly more than just a large snake. Also known as a cockatrice, it has existed in legend for centuries. Rowling is just having fun in *Beasts* when she credits a Greek wizard named Herpo the Foul with breeding the first basilisk. *Herpein* is a Greek word meaning 'to creep' that came to be a word describing snakes. The study of reptiles such as snakes is now called herpetology.

Basilisks,
from an early
woodcut and a
later engraving.

However, just as she suggests, by legend the basilisk was said to be the offspring of a rooster or hen mated with a snake or toad. Some artists followed that description literally, and drew strange beasts combining features from

those animals. But more often the basilisk was portrayed as a serpent with a crown or a white spot on his head. Cobras, which have such marks, may be the origin of the basilisk legend.

The basilisk was reported to be deadly even from afar. The Roman naturalist Pliny said, 'He kills all trees and shrubs, not only those he touches but all he breathes upon. He burns the grass, and breaks stones, so venomous and deadly is he.'

Some sources describe three varieties: the golden basilisk could poison with a look; another sparked fire; a third, like the famous snaky hair of Medusa in Greek mythology, caused such horror that victims were petrified.

William Shakespeare even mentioned a basilisk in his play *Richard III*. The evil title character kills his brother then immediately flatters his brother's widow by mentioning her beautiful eyes. But she replies, 'Would they were a basilisk's, to strike thee dead!'

HOW TO FIGHT A BASILISK

A basilisk controlled by Lord Voldemort slinks through Hogwarts in *Chamber*, almost killing Harry and his friends. Fawkes, Professor Dumbledore's pet phoenix, attacks the monster. That also matches legend. A bird – the rooster – is fatal to the beast. In the Middle Ages travellers carried roosters as protection against basilisks.

Humans who looked at the snaky head of **Medusa** were turned to stone. The hero Perseus slayed it by looking only at its reflection in his metal shield, just as Hermione avoids the full force of the basilisk's power because she only sees its reflection.

See also:
Beasts
Nagini
Spiders

Which 'Fantastic Beasts' Come from Legend?

MANY OF THE CREATURES IN THE TEXTBOOK *Fantastic Beasts and Where to Find Them* are known in our world as well as Harry's, even if they are legendary. Here are some of the stories from which J. K. Rowling drew:

RED CAP

According to *Fantastic Beasts and Where to Find Them*, Red Caps 'live in holes on old battlegrounds or wherever human blood has been spilled . . . [and] will attempt to bludgeon [muggles] to death on dark nights.' This creature has long existed in the legends of England and Scotland, neighbours who fought many gruesome wars. He is also known as Bloody Cap or Red Comb. His cap is red because he uses it to catch the blood of his victims.

British legends also tell of a **Blue Cap**, a spirit who helped miners.

RAMORA

True to a legend that goes back thousands of

35

The author of *Beasts*, Newton ('Newt') Artemis Fido Scamander, has a name filled with puns.

Newts are small salamanders (see page 37).

Artemis was the Greek goddess of hunting – good for an animal scholar.

Fido, from the Latin *fidus* ('faithful'), is a common name for pets.

'Scamander' means to wander in a winding way, as Newt did while exploring.

years, Rowling says this fish – which does exist and which we know as the remora – has the power to stop ships. In fact, the name remora comes from the Latin word for 'delay'. Using a suction cup on its head, it attaches itself to ships and sharks in order to feed on scraps. Also known as the Mora and Echeneis, its strength had already been exaggerated by the first century AD, when Pliny the Elder wrote, 'Winds howl, storms rage: this fish commands their frenzied force to be still, stopping ships with a great power, greater than any anchor. Humankind is a vain weak creature when its giant warships are stopped by a tiny fish!' Pliny claimed the ship of Marc Antony was anchored by remoras during the Battle of Actium, causing him to lose the battle and changing the course of Roman history.

HIPPOCAMPUS

This sea horse gets its name from the Greek words for horse (*hippos*) and sea monster (*kampos*). It is also called the Hydrippus (the Greek word for 'water' is *hydro*.) The chariot of the Greek sea-god Poseidon is pulled by hippocamps.

A book called the *Physiologus*, written about the second century AD, says some legends deemed the Hippocampus 'the leader of all fishes'. Judaism and Christianity were on the rise at the time, and the Hippocampus was imagined to be a prophet or guide similar to Moses. It was said to lead other fish to a Holy Land (or Holy Sea, that is) where a special golden fish lives: 'When the fish of the sea have met together and gathered themselves into flocks, they go in search of the Hydrippus; and when they have found him, he turns himself towards the East, and they all follow him, all the fish from the North and from the South; and they draw near to the golden fish, the Hydrippus leading them. And, when the Hydrippus and all the fish are arrived, they greet the golden fish as their King.'

Hippocampus, from a Dutch woodcut.

SALAMANDER

In *Fantastic Beasts and Where to Find Them* Rowling says these are 'fire-dwelling' lizards that live 'only as long as the fire from which they sprang burns'. This legend goes back thousands of years. The Greek philosopher Aristotle wrote in the fourth century BC that 'the fact that certain animals cannot be burnt is evidenced by the salamander, which puts out a fire by crawling through it.' It could do this because it was said to be extremely cold. Almost a thousand years later St Isidore, Bishop of

Salamander in flames, from a family crest.

Seville, agreed that the salamander 'lives in the midst of flames without pain and without being consumed', adding, 'amid all poisons its power is the greatest. Other poisonous animals strike individuals, but this slays many at the same time by crawling up a tree and infecting the fruit, killing all those who eat it.'

Some legends said the **salamander** lived in cocoons that were used to spin a fireproof fabric. Instead of being washed in water, clothes made from it were supposedly cleaned with fire.

ERKLING

Rowling has transposed a few letters in the name of the Erl King or Erl König ('elf king') of German legend. Otherwise, her description holds true. It is an evil creature in the Black Forest of Germany that tries to snatch children. In Johann Wolfgang von Goethe's poem 'Erl King' it calls out to a young boy who is travelling through the woods with his father:

> *'Oh, come, thou dear infant! Oh, come thou with me!*
> *Full many a game I will play there with thee.'*

Although the boy tries to warn his father (who can't hear the Erl King), the poem ends badly. Like legends of grindylows in England and kappas in Japan, the story of the Erl King was concocted by parents to prevent children from wandering.

The description of the Chimaera in *Beasts*, odd as it sounds, is true to the early Greek legend of a monster with the head of a lion, the body of a goat, and the tail of a dragon or serpent. (In another version the heads of all three animals were on a lion's body. Yet other versions added wings.) It is a sibling of both the Sphinx and Cerberus, the three-headed dog that guarded the Underworld.

In *Fantastic Beasts and Where to Find Them* Rowling casually mentions 'there is only one known instance of the successful slaying of a Chimaera and the unlucky wizard concerned fell to his death from his winged horse.' She is playing with the original legend, in which the monster was slain by the hero Bellerophon, who rode the winged horse Pegasus. Bellerophon survived that battle; but in a later adventure, when he arrogantly attempted to ride the horse to Mount Olympus, home of the gods, Zeus punished him by throwing him off Pegasus and crippling him.

The term 'chimaera' has come to mean something (usually a living creature) created by humans by artificially combining things that occur in nature.

KELPIE

As described in *Beasts*, this Celtic water demon is usually seen as a horse with a mane of green rushes. It lures people on to its back, then drags them into deep water. As Rowling says, bridling a kelpie will subdue it. Because it is supernaturally strong, it can do the work of many horses.

SELKIES AND MERROWS

See also:
Boggarts
Cornish Pixies
Grindylows
Kappas
Merpeople
Unicorns
Veela

In the entry for merpeople in *Beasts*, Rowling mentions selkies and merrows. These are specific sorts of merpeople known in Britain. The selkies are seal people of the country's northern islands. They can assume very beautiful human forms, but must resume their seal form in the water. To kill a selkie is to invite a disastrous storm. Merrows are from Ireland. The women are beautiful but the men are quite ugly. They are said to have magic hats, and if a human can steal the hat the merrow will not be able to return to the sea.

Why Would Sirius Black Become a Black Dog?

SIRIUS BLACK, HARRY'S GODFATHER, IS A fugitive from the Ministry of Magic, which mistakenly believes he is a Death Eater. He was able to escape Azkaban because he is an Animagus. He changed into his dog form, squeezed through the bars of his cell, and swam to his freedom.

THE DOG STAR

As an Animagus form, a black dog suits him perfectly. The name 'Sirius' comes from the name of a star often referred to as the Dog Star. It has that nickname because it is in the constellation known as the Great Dog. (The star was given the name 'Sirius' because it is the brightest star in the sky. The Greek word *seirios* means 'burning'.)

That star has great significance in the magical world. As the symbol of the goddess Isis,

The Egyptian goddess **Isis**.

it was central to the religion and philosophy of Egypt, where most magic originated.

The Egyptians used Sirius to set their calendar, because its movements are linked to the seasons. On the first day of summer, it rises just before the sun. That was New Year's Day in ancient Egypt. It forecast the annual flooding of the Nile River, which gave vital nourishment to the growing fields. We refer to the long, hot days of summer now as 'dog days' because Sirius marks their arrival.

According to the Egyptians, Sirius was not merely significant to life on Earth. The star was where the souls of humans travelled after death. The star was so important that temples were built to align with its path across the sky. An archaeologist determined that the long tunnels or airshafts in the Great Pyramid make the stars visible in daytime, and that the view

Magical creature expert Carol Rose says some black dogs, such as two supposedly living near Somerset, England, are said to guard treasures or holy places.

is that part of the sky where Sirius appears. One Egyptologist says those shafts were meant to guide one's soul to Sirius.

PADFOOT

The Animagus form of a black dog is appropriate to Sirius Black in more than name alone. Magical black dogs appear mysteriously throughout Europe and North America. There have been many sightings in Britain, where they are known by names like Black Shuck (from the Anglo-Saxon *scucca*, meaning 'demon'), Old Shuck, Shucky Dog, the Shug Monster and Shag Dog. The residents of Staffordshire gave it the name Sirius uses: Padfoot.

Some say the dogs guard churchyards or certain roads; others say they roam the countryside at night. Eyewitnesses say they appear suddenly, sometimes right alongside a person walking alone. They tend to be larger than usual dogs. They may vanish in an instant, or slowly fade from view while standing still. Occasionally they appear without heads. Their eyes are almost always described as huge and 'blazing'. Surprisingly, they tend to be silent.

Scholars were once convinced that the black dog was the preferred form of the Devil. Even among people with less anxious minds,

In *Harry Potter and the Order of the Phoenix* Rowling reveals that names taken from astronomy are a Black family tradition: Sirius's cousin **Andromeda** is named for a constellation; her sister **Bellatrix** is named for a bright star in the constellation Orion; and Sirius's late brother **Regulus** is named for the brightest star in the constellation Leo.

It was once
believed that
the Greek
goddess of
sorcery, **Hecate**
(HEK-uh-tuh),
roamed rural
Britain with two
black dogs as
companions.
She was
thought to be
invisible, so two
black dogs with
no owner in
sight were a
bad sign.

See also:
Animagus
Egypt

black dogs are widely feared. Many consider them an omen of death. This is precisely what Professor Trelawney tells Harry his early sightings of Sirius mean. (She refers to the black dog as the Grim, another common name.)

The eyewitness reports go back many hundreds of years. One vivid account from 1577 describes the arrival of a black dog in church: 'There appeared in a most horrible form a dog of a black colour, together with fearful flashes of fire which made some in the assembly think doomsday was come. This dog, or the Devil in such a likeness, ran the length of the church with great swiftness and incredible haste, passed between two persons as they were kneeling and wrung the necks of them both at one instant.'

That may have been an especially horrible incident. Not every encounter is so awful. In more recent sightings the black dog seems to have become less malevolent. Simon Sherwood, an expert on the subject, says, 'There is rather more evidence that black dogs are friendly (or at least harmless) than that they are dangerous. Indeed the dogs are often positively helpful.'

Why Does the Black Family Appear on a Tapestry?

CONSIDERING J. K. ROWLING'S INVENTIONS include moving photographs and talking paintings, some readers of *Phoenix* may guess that Rowling created the Black family tapestry at Grimmauld Place entirely from her imagination. But ornate storytelling tapestries have existed for thousands of years, going back to early Egypt and Asia. In Europe all the great medieval castles had tapestries, which were needed to help keep out draughts and to keep in heat. Naturally, wealthier people had more decorative tapestries, and the wealthiest had versions specially designed to show a family crest or a scene from family history. Churches also had them.

Some tapestries were woven from designs drawn by famous artists. Raphael (1483–1520), one of the greatest artists of the Renaissance, was asked by Pope Leo X to design tapestries for the Vatican showing scenes from the Bible.

'Toujours Pur', the Black family motto, means 'Always Pure' in French. Of course it refers to pure wizard blood, the obsession of so many generations of Blacks before Sirius.

45

The art of telling stories with tapestries never disappeared. Artist William Morris designed some in the 1800s. More recently, the Bayeux Tapestry inspired the Overlord Embroidery in Portsmouth, England. It shows the Second World War effort to send armies back across the English Channel that William I crossed in 1066.

Right: a detail from the Bayeux Tapestry

Tapestries were also designed to celebrate military victories. The Bayeux Tapestry, perhaps the most famous of all, tells the story of King William's conquest of England in 1066. Blenheim Palace in Oxfordshire, England, has a tapestry that shows the 1st Duke of Marlborough's victory over the French at the Battle of Blenheim in 1704 (for which he was given the land and the funds for the palace). Many, however, are symbolic. The complexity of the Unicorn Tapestries, seven works that portray a hunt for a unicorn, have prompted countless theories about what the artist had in mind.

Which Creature Doesn't Know When to Say Goodbye?

SOME MAGICAL CREATURES CAN BE MORE dangerous than others. A boggart might seem dangerous at first, because, as J. K. Rowling's Hermione explains in *Harry Potter and the Prisoner of Azkaban*, it can 'take the shape of whatever it thinks will frighten us most'. But more than anything else, boggarts are annoying.

These are the same creatures known as 'bogeys' or 'bogeymen' in the United States, 'bogle' in Scotland, and 'Boggelmann' or 'Butzemann' in Germany. Sometimes said to be mistreated spirits that have become malevolent, boggarts love mischief and usually aren't very harmful. They like to come out at night, when they can be most convincing.

Often they are house spirits, and in those cases the only way to get rid of them is to move. This is easier said than done, as a

From the words *bogey* and *boggart* we also get names of less frightening annoyances like 'bugaboo' and 'bugbear'.

boggart will sometimes take the trouble to move with a household it finds particularly entertaining. The more frustrated the family becomes, the more fun the boggart has.

Harry faces boggarts in *Azkaban* and in the maze in *Goblet*. He defeats them with advice from Professor Lupin that sounds like what children in our world have been told for centuries: 'The thing that really finishes a boggart is laughter,' (*Harry Potter and the Prisoner of Azkaban* by J. K. Rowling). Of course, this is easier for wizards, who can simply use the Riddikulus charm to turn the boggart into something funny. Yet even then it's not always easy. If you face a truly cruel boggart like the one Mrs Weasley encounters in *Phoenix*, it can be hard to keep calm. Some jokes just aren't funny.

See also:

Beasts
Cornish Pixies
Goblins
Trolls
Veela

Have Witches Always Flown on Broomsticks?

B Y LEGEND, BROOMSTICKS ARE THE MOST common means of transportation for witches. A popular American writer of the nineteenth century, Oliver Wendell Holmes, penned this rhyme on the subject:

> In Essex county there's many a roof
> Well known to him of the cloven hoof;
> The small square windows are full in view
> Which the midnight hags went sailing
>   through,
> On their well-trained broomsticks
>   mounted high,
> Seen like shadows against the sky;
> Crossing the track of owls and bats,
> Hugging before them their coal-black cats.

Women were more likely than men to use this means of travel, perhaps because the broom is used for domestic chores, which men avoided. Sorcerers, when they did fly, usually rode on pitchforks. For reasons never explained, witches in Europe and America were seen flying more often than those in Britain.

Witches were rumoured to rub their broomsticks with a magical ointment to make them fly. Then, according to legend, they rode straight out of the chimney. This colourful exaggeration derived from the real practice of pushing a broom up a chimney to let neighbours know one was away from home. Still, it sounds a bit like travelling by floo powder.

If villagers suspected that witches were flying about they would ring church bells, which reportedly had the power to knock witches off broomsticks.

Witches were sometimes accused of flying out to sea to create a storm.

One witch has emerged from the chimney on her broomstick, and another is halfway up it, in this sixteenth-century woodcut.

Why Would Mundungus Fletcher Steal Cauldrons?

CAULDRONS ARE IMPORTANT ENOUGH TO be required for all first-year students at Hogwarts, and, as we learn in *Phoenix*, valuable enough for Mundungus Fletcher to trade in stolen ones. It's the same in our world. Cauldrons are one of the oldest and most widely known symbols of magic. They are more rooted in history and myth than flying broomsticks, and are thought to have even greater powers.

RIVER OF LIFE

Hogwarts wizards use cauldrons to mix potions, the use we now think of most often. Yet in early myth and legend they have other powers. In Scandinavian mythology, a magical cauldron called Hvergelmer lies deep in the Scandinavian version of the underworld, a frozen land of everlasting night known as Niflheim. Dangerous rivers flow from the

What sort of name is **Mundungus**? The perfect name for someone who smells as bad he does. It's an old word for stinky tobacco or anything that reeks like garbage. When Mundungus lights a pipe in *Phoenix* it smells as though he is smoking socks.

cauldron, making wind, rain, snow and ice. Poison that flowed from it formed a giant, and from him the Earth was then formed.

The magical power of cauldrons also goes back to early mythology. Medea, the grand sorceress of Greek mythology who helped Jason win the golden fleece, used her cauldron to perform her greatest feat. She boiled a brew of exotic plants gathered from all over the world, along with the wings of an owl, parts of a werewolf, the skin of a snake, and other delicacies, and, 'with these and a thousand other nameless ingredients' she accomplished 'a deed beyond mortal power': slitting the throat of Jason's elderly father and filling his veins with the potion, she restored his youth. Even the gods on Olympus were impressed.

It's no coincidence that at the climax of *Goblet* Voldemort attempts his own version of Medea's recipe.

TOO MANY COOKS SPOIL THE SOUP
Celtic lore had its own version of the Medea myth: Bran the Blessed, the warrior giant, had a cauldron with the power to bring the dead back to life. Along with the lore there were rituals known as the 'cauldron mysteries'. These secret rites dealt with the great questions of death and rebirth. There is evidence that

'Alas, poor man; his eyes are sunk, and his hands shrivelled; his legs dwindled, and his back bowed: pray, pray, for a metamorphosis. Change thy shape and shake off age; get thee **Medea's kettle** and be boiled anew.'

William Congreve
Love for Love, 1695
(Act IV, sc. xv)

humans were sacrificed in cauldrons as part of some rituals.

Perhaps the most famous Celtic cauldron legend is the story of Cerridwen and Taliesen. In old myths, Cerridwen is a goddess of magic and wisdom; in legends from the Christian era, she is a gifted sorceress; in both she has a special cauldron kept hot by a fire fed by the breath of muses, the goddesses of the arts. To give her son wisdom, Cerridwen decided to mix a special brew. Made from magical plants and the foam of the sea, it had to boil for a year and a day just to yield three drops. One day the boy hired to stir the cauldron accidentally splattered some on his hand and licked it.

British doctor Francis Potter (1594–1678) was inspired by the myth of Medea and Jason's father to attempt the first **blood** transfusion.

Woodcut from a 1582 German book warning against magic.

He became smarter in an instant. But being smarter, he knew Cerridwen would be furious. Fortunately, he had also gained so much

People once
believed that
witches flew in
cauldrons.

knowledge he turned himself into a hare to run away; unfortunately, Cerridwen turned herself into a greyhound. He became a fish; she became an otter. He became a rabbit; she became a hawk. Finally he changed himself into a grain of wheat to hide in a field. But she found him, and, changing herself into a hen, ate him. Nine months later she gave birth to a new boy, brilliant and beautiful, who went on to become a great poet named Taliesen. His special gifts came directly from the muses that helped to heat Cerridwen's cauldron.

See
Animagus

You might guess that Mundungus could find something more worthwhile to peddle than stolen pots. But in Harry's world as in ours, very little is valued more than divine wisdom and eternal youth.

Why Do Centaurs Avoid Humans?

CENTAURS ARE MYTHICAL BEASTS WITH THE legs and bodies of horses, but with human torsos, arms, and heads. In *Fantastic Beasts and Where to Find Them*, J. K. Rowling says 'they prefer to live apart from wizards and Muggles alike.' This feeling is echoed in *Phoenix* when Bane feuds with Firenze for being friendly with humans. This fits the ancient legends. According to those stories, centaurs come from the mountains of Greece, where their relations with the local people were rather mixed. Because some centaurs were fond of wine, they tended to be boisterous, wild and quick to anger. They fought many battles with humans. The most famous skirmish followed a wedding at which the centaurs, as usual, had celebrated a little too enthusiastically. They tried to carry off the bride, which led to a great war. (The centaurs

Centaur, from a second-century AD sarcophagus.

lost.) Scenes from that war were a favourite decoration of Greek potters.

However, some ancient centaurs were recognized to be as noble as Firenze. In fact Firenze's surprise appearance as a Hogwarts teacher in *Phoenix* is connected to mythology. The Greek centaur Chiron, having been taught arts such as medicine and hunting by the gods Apollo and Artemis, founded a school where he taught some of the great heroes of the time, including Achilles and Odysseus.

The centaur **Nessos**, foe of the hero Hercules, as pictured on a Greek amphora (vase) made in the seventh century BC.

LOST IN THE STARS

Although Chiron was immortal, a wound from a poisoned arrow threatened to cause him unceasing agony. Instead, he chose death. But Zeus, in recognition of Chiron's benevolence, placed him in the stars as the constellation Sagittarius. Another constellation, Centaurus, is one of the most visible in the Southern Hemisphere. These heavenly connections may explain why the centaurs who live in the Forbidden Forest near Hogwarts – Firenze, Ronan, and Bane – look to the stars to read the future.

What's the Favourite Trick of Cornish Pixies?

PIXIES ARE ENERGETIC HOUSEHOLD SPIRITS from the legends of Cornwall and the south-west of England. Most stories depict them dressed in green, wearing a pointed cap. They have youthful faces and many have red hair. J. K. Rowling departs from tradition in *Harry Potter and the Chamber of Secrets* and *Fantastic Beasts and Where to Find Them*, describing them as 'electric blue and about eight inches high.'

In folklore, pixies are often said to act like the house elves of Harry's world. They can be quite helpful but will disappear if given a gift of clothes. Unlike house elves, who are happy to do all the work, pixies will nip at lazy members of a household.

Pixies love to dance under the moonlight. At times they also take horses from stalls and ride them all night, returning them exhausted – and with mysteriously knotted manes – in

It is said that pixies live in caves or burial mounds and come out only at night.

the morning. But their favourite activity is to lead travellers astray. People who have lost their way (or are in any way bewildered or confused) are said to be 'pixie-led'. This disorienting spell may be broken by taking off one's jacket and putting it on again, inside out.

Leading travellers off a path is a trick often played by another English spirit mentioned in *Azkaban*, the hinkypunk. Because it seems more like a misty cloud than a solid creature, some people call it the will-o'-the-wisp.

See also:

Beasts

Boggarts

Why Would Voldemort Put the Dark Mark on Death Eaters?

Dark Mark

T HE DARK MARK IS THE FEARSOME SIGN OF Lord Voldemort. After the Quidditch World Cup in Rowling's *Harry Potter and the Goblet of Fire*, 'Something vast, green, and glittering erupted from the patch of darkness . . . It was a colossal skull, comprised of what looked like emerald stars, with a serpent protruding from its mouth like a tongue.' The symbol also appears on the arms of Voldemort's followers, growing more visible as Voldemort gains strength and draws near.

The Dark Mark is Voldemort's version of the Devil's Mark, a notion from the Middle Ages. According to one medieval demonologist, 'the Devil makes a mark on them, especially those whose allegiance he suspects. The mark varies in shape and size; sometimes it is like a hare, sometimes like the foot of a toad, sometimes like a spider, a puppy, or a dormouse. It is imprinted on the most secret parts

'Morsmordre,' the command that makes the Dark Mark appear, means 'take a bite out of death' in French, making it a fitting call for Death Eaters.

of the body; men may have it under their eyelids or armpits, on the lips or shoulders; women generally have it on their breasts or private parts. The stamp that makes these marks is nothing less than the Devil's talon.'

Witch hunters often declared scars, birthmarks, warts, or other blemishes to be the Devil's Mark. Accused witches were shaved completely so that every bit of their bodies could be examined.

In addition to the Devil's Mark, witch hunters would look for a Witch's Mark. This was a less serious matter – only the Devil's Mark signified a special pact, such as the bond between Voldemort and the Death Eaters – but it could still be fatal for the accused person. Every witch was believed to have one. Any blemish, like a mole or large freckle, might be identified as such

Sometimes the Witch's Mark was said to be a spot of skin that did not bleed and where no pain could be felt, so accused witches were pricked with pins (called bodkins) as a test. Often, witch hunters were paid only if they found a witch; so many cheated. For instance, they used special bodkins, similar to the trick knives used in magicians' acts today. The sharp stem would disappear into the handle when pressed against someone, so it would not puncture the skin.

Bodkins like these were used to prick alleged witches, to test for the **Devil's Mark**. This illustration shows a trick bodkin. Its blade collapses into the handle.

See also:
Broomsticks
Voldemort

What Story Began With a Dark and Stormy Knight?

J. K. ROWLING'S PREPARATION FOR WRITING Harry's adventures included creating a history for the Death Eaters, which she says were originally known as the Knights of Walpurgis. The name is a pun, a reversal of 'Walpurgis Night', the name of an old witches' holiday celebrating springtime. Walpurgis Night was the night of 30 April (by our modern calendar), the eve of the May Day festival. That date is exactly six months from Hallowe'en, and the two holidays were related in theme. One ushered in the growing season, one marked its passing. On Walpurgis Night as on Hallowe'en, witches and demons supposedly ran wild.

These 1545 woodcuts claim to show a witch and wizards riding to a gathering.

The holiday was celebrated throughout northern Europe and in Britain under various names. 'Walpurgis Night' is a translation of the German name. It refers to Saint Walpurgis (also 'Walburga'), a nun who helped introduce

61

Christianity to Germany in the 700s. (The holiday came to have her name by chance. The day chosen to honour her coincided with the the traditional spring festival. Walpurgis herself had nothing to do with witchcraft.)

The centre of the German celebration was a famous mountain called the Brocken in northern Germany. Witches and demons were said to gather there. Johann Wolfgang von Goethe's classic work *Faust*, about a man who sells his soul to the devil, includes a Walpurgis Night scene on the Brocken. Many magical creatures including griffins, sirens and phoenixes join the devil, who announces,

> *I'm like a tom-cat in a thievish vein,*
> *That up fire-ladders tall and steep,*
> *And round the walls doth slyly creep;*
> *. . . Thus through my limbs already burns*
> *The glorious Walpurgis night!*
> *After to-morrow it returns.*

It's easy to see how the rogue witches on the Brocken might make someone think of the Death Eaters. Perhaps that also explains why Rowling placed Durmstrang, which is sympathetic to Voldemort, not far away.

Walpurgis was actually a Briton, from Devonshire, Wessex. She was the daughter of a Saxon king and the niece of St Boniface, the Apostle of Germany. Because of her intelligence and skill, the mixed monastery at Heidenheim, Germany, where she was abbess, was highly influential.

'BURNING OUT THE WITCHES'

Fear of Walpurgis Night created its own rituals. One historian describes how people rid themselves of witches after that hellish night:

> On the last three days of April all the houses are cleansed and fumigated with juniper berries and rue. On May Day, when the evening bell has rung and the twilight is falling, the ceremony of 'Burning out the Witches' begins. Men and boys make a racket with whips, bells, pots, and pans; the women carry censers [incense holders]; the dogs are unchained and run barking and yelping about. As soon as the church bells begin to ring, the bundles of twigs, fastened on poles, are set on fire and the incense is ignited. Then all the house-bells and dinner-bells are rung, pots and pans are clashed, dogs bark, every one must make a noise. And amid this hubbub all scream at the pitch of their voices: *'Witch flee, flee from here, or it will go ill with thee.'* Then they run seven times round the houses, the yards, and the village. So the witches are smoked out of their lurking-places and driven away.

Some northern European countries still celebrate Walpurgis Night, though without the worry about witches.

That description might be funny if it were a scene about Muggles in a Harry Potter book, but as an account of real life it sounds ridiculous. On the other hand, consider this: In Britain, where the festival was known as Beltane, there is evidence that the celebrations included sacrifices of animals and even humans. The Death Eaters would have liked that.

See
Dark Mark
Umbridge,
Dolores

Why Would Chocolate Help After Escaping a Dementor?

DEMENTORS, AS EVERY HARRY POTTER fan knows, are deadly magical creatures. J. K. Rowling introduces them in *Harry Potter and the Prisoner of Azkaban:* faceless, wearing shapeless cloaks that cover skin that is 'greyish, slimy-looking, and scabbed', they 'drain peace, hope, and happiness out of the air around them'.

ROWLING'S EXPLANATION

Rowling has told an interviewer that Dementors represent the mental illness known as depression. She said the choice was deliberate, and based on her own encounter with the disease, which she called the worst experience she has ever endured. Much worse, she says, than merely feeling 'sad' – a perfectly normal emotion – depression is an actual loss of feeling. That is just what happens to humans in the presence of Dementors. Dumbledore hates

Dementors, because they aren't satisfied until they've consumed all hope and feeling.

One can't help but notice that the remedy offered to lighten the effects of Dementors is chocolate, which doctors say can make depressed people feel better. The chocolate has some of the same effects as the medicine that doctors prescribe. Of course, chocolate does seem to be a cure for nearly every ill in Harry's world.

One also can't ignore the connection between Rowling's own experience and the uncomfortable moment in *Phoenix* when Harry sees Neville Longbottom and Neville's grandmother, who are visiting Neville's parents at St Mungo's Hospital. Mr and Mrs Longbottom are in the hospital because Voldemort's attack damaged their minds. Neville is ashamed; Harry is embarrassed on Neville's behalf; but Neville's grandmother, older and wiser, is matter-of-fact about the whole thing, which makes it much easier on everyone.

Appropriately, Madam **Pomfrey's** name comes from a sweet. Pomfret cakes are discs of liquorice from Pontefract, Yorkshire. A surprising fact: the area's reknowned liquorice was first cultivated to be used as a medicine.

Does Dumbledore Trust Divination or Doesn't He?

SYBILL TRELAWNEY DOESN'T GET A LOT OF respect. Professor McGonagall sneers after learning Trelawney has predicted Harry will die during this third year at Hogwarts: 'Sibyll Trelawney has predicted the death of one student a year since she arrived at this school. None of them has died yet.'(*Harry Potter and the Prisoner of Azkaban* by J. K. Rowling) Dumbledore did not want to hire her because he didn't think she had a gift for divination.

Yet the whole plot of *Harry Potter and the Order of the Phoenix* centres on a Trelawney prophecy that seems to be accurate. So does Dumbledore believe in divination or not?

PERFECT VISION

Dumbledore, it seems, draws a line between divination and prophecy. The difference is important.

Some types of
divination:

Belomancy:
study of the
flight of arrows

Bibliomancy:
random passage
in a book

Dactylomancy:
swinging of a
suspended ring

Daphnomancy:
the crackling of
burning laurel

Geloscopy:
laughter

Lampadomancy:
a lamp flame

Libranomancy:
incense smoke

Divination is the interpretation of signs and actions to predict the future or look into the past, or, sometimes, just find lost objects. Many methods are used. The Romans favoured augury, interpreting the flight of birds. Other cultures examined the insides of sacrificed animals. Some people still 'read' the arrangement of tea leaves or coffee grinds left in a cup.

Dumbledore doesn't trust this kind of divination. People see what they like in the flight of birds, which isn't influenced by mystical powers.

A true 'seer' – someone who can see the future – is said to have a 'gift' of prophecy. Like all gifts, it must come from somebody. Prophecy is said to come from the gods, who don't communicate through tea leaves. In the ancient world, seers called 'oracles' lived at temples so they could contact gods. The most famous temple, at Delphi, Greece, endured for twelve centuries and was linked to various gods: an ancient earth mother; a later earth goddess, Gaea; Dionysus, the god of fertility and wine; and Apollo, the god most associated with prophecy. The priestesses went into a trance so the gods could speak through them.

ALL IN THE FAMILY

So why does Dumbledore give Trelawney a chance? Rowling explains in *Harry Potter and the Order of the Phoenix* that Trelawney is descended from 'a very famous, very gifted Seer' and Dumbledore wanted to be respectful. The name of that ancestor, Cassandra Trelawney, says it all. Cassandra is the name of the most famous seer in Greek myth, a woman who received her gift directly from the god Apollo. He loved her, and promised her the gift of prophecy if she would love him. But after he made her clairvoyant she changed her mind. As punishment, Apollo declared that no one would ever believe her predictions. This caused her a lot of grief, most notably during the Trojan War. She was the daughter of the king of Troy, and was in the city when Greek soldiers tried to invade. After it seemed the Greeks had given up and left behind the gift of a large wooden horse, she warned her father not to celebrate, and to leave the horse outside the city walls. But because of Apollo's curse her father did not heed her. Of course, Greek soldiers were hidden inside the horse. When it was inside the city they slipped out and took over.

Perhaps the strange voice Trelawney used when making the prediction to Dumbledore – not her usual fortune-telling voice, Harry notices when Dumbledore shows him the memory – might have made Dumbledore wonder if Trelawney's great-great-grandmother

Lithomancy: gemstones

Metoposcopy: forehead wrinkles

Palmistry: lines of the palm

Phrenology: shape of the skull

Some people **burn sage** to tell the future, as Rowling's Centaurs do in *Phoenix*; and of course many people follow the stars with **astrology**, as the Centaurs do in *Stone*.

The divination
textbook used
at Hogwarts
was written by
a '**Cassandra
Vablatsky**'; her
last name refers
to a real woman
who claimed
psychic powers.
Helena Petrovna
Blavatsky
founded the
Theosophical
Society, whose
aims include
'investigating
unexplained
laws of nature
and the powers
latent in
humanity' – in
other words,
magic.

See also:
**Centaurs
Runes**

was speaking through her. Ignoring such a warning would not have been wise.

Not coincidentally, Sybill Trelawney's first name also comes from famous prophets of mythology. The books containing the predictions of the Sybils were the most valuable volumes in the Roman Empire. Like Sybill Trelawney, the Roman Sybils were inclined to make predictions – often dreadful ones – without being asked. Of course Prof. Trelawney will never live up to the reputation of the Roman Sybils. One correct prophecy is not much of a record, even if it is important.

Perhaps Dumbledore's scepticism about divination can be traced back to J. K. Rowling. She does seem ambivalent about it. Hermione finds it 'very woolly', yet is fond of arithmancy, which is divination from numbers. Though centaurs in the Forbidden Forest read the future in the stars, they seem wise. They also burn leaves to watch the smoke, as Firenze explains to Harry's class in *Phoenix*, but even Firenze reveals his doubts about that. Maybe Rowling feels as Dumbledore explains to Harry in *Harry Potter and the Prisoner of Azkaban*: 'The consequences of our actions are always so complicated, so diverse, that predicting the future is a very difficult business indeed.'

Which Creature Is Fit for a King?

DRAGONS (FROM THE LATIN *DRACO* – JUST like Draco Malfoy) are probably the best-known magical creatures in literature. Usually dangerous and terrifying, they are often the most challenging foe a hero can face. Literary critics John Clute and John Grant note this rule of ancient epics: 'To kill a dragon is often to become a king.' As a result the dragon is the symbol of many real and fictional kings, including the legendary King Arthur, whose last name, Pendragon, means 'head of the dragon' or 'chief dragon'. His golden helmet bore a dragon design.

However, as some heroes discover, dragons are often misunderstood. Though they can be frightening, they can also be benevolent.

J. R. R. Tolkien, author of *The Lord of the Rings*, called dragons the trademark of fairy tales and myths.

UGLINESS IS ONLY SKIN DEEP
Many people fear dragons simply because of

their appearance. This description from about AD 600 was taken very seriously:

> The dragon is the largest of all serpents and of all living things upon earth. It has a small face and narrow blow-holes through which it draws its breath and thrusts out its tongue. Being dragged from caves it rushes into the air, and the air is thrown into commotion on account of it. And it has its strength not in its teeth but in its tail, and it is dangerous for its stroke, rather than for its jaws. It is harmless in the way of poison, but poison is not necessary for it to cause death, because it kills whatever it has entangled in its folds. And from it the elephant is not safe because of its size. It grows in Ethiopia and in India, in the very burning of perennial heat.

Dragons on family crests.

It is easy to see why the dragon is often a symbol of destruction. That idea goes back thousands of years. In the New Testament, the Lord warns, 'I will make Jerusalem heaps, and a den of dragons; and I will make the cities of Judah desolate, without an inhabitant.'

BRITISH DRAGONS

Dragons play a big part in the legends of Harry's homeland. For instance, they foretold one of the most important moments in British history. According to an official chronicle, the year AD 793 began with 'dreadful fore-warnings over the land of the Northumbrians, terrifying the people most woefully. Whirlwinds and immense sheets of light rushed through the air, and fiery dragons flew across the sky. These tremendous tokens were soon followed by a great famine: and not long after, invading heathens made lamentable havoc in the church of God in Holy-island [Lindisfarne]'. Those 'invading heathens' were Norsemen from Scandinavia. True to what

In both Europe and Asia, comets and meteors were sometimes taken to be flying, fire-breathing dragons.

had been foretold, their ships were decorated to look like dragons. They continued to dominate Britain for hundreds of years.

Not surprisingly, the saint later adopted as the patron of England, St George, is famous for slaying a dragon – symbolically defeating the foreigners. In *The Faerie Queen*, a famous poem written during the reign of Queen Elizabeth I, poet Edmund Spenser describes the dragon faced by the 'Red-Cross Knight':

> *His body was monstrous, horrible, and vast,*
> *Swollen with wrath and poison and with*
> *   bloody gore;*
> *And over all with brazen scales was armed,*
> *Like plated coat of steel, that nothing*
> *   might pierce it,*
> *Nor could his body be harmed with dint of*
> *   sword, nor push of pointed spear.*
> *His wings were like two sails in which the*
> *   hollow wind*
> *Is gathered full, and work speedy way.*
> *His huge long tail, wound up in hundred*
> *   folds,*
> *Spread across his long back.*
> *Spotted with scales of red and black,*
> *It sweeps all the land behind him,*
> *And at the end two stingers:*
> *Both deadly sharp – sharper than steel, by far.*

Legend has it that St George slayed the dragon at what is now **Dragon's Hill** in Berkshire, England. It's said no grass can grow where the dragon's blood was spilled.

His deep devouring jaws
Gaped wide, like the grisly mouth of hell,
And in either jaw were three rows of iron teeth
In which, still trickling blood and raw guts,
Recently devoured bodies did appear.

THE GOOD SIDE OF DRAGONS

But dragons are not always enemies of humans. Especially in Asia, the dragon is benevolent – though sometimes bossy. Most importantly, it is a symbol of leadership.

The Asian calendar is divided into twelve-year cycles, with each of those years associated with a particular animal. People born in the Year of the Dragon are said to be the best leaders, combining a strong will with a generous nature.

WHAT'S INSIDE A DRAGON'S BRAIN?

Some authorities say a magical gemstone, called draconite, can be found inside a dragon's head: 'There is cut out of the dragon's brain a stone, but it is not a stone unless it be taken while the dragon is alive. For if the dragon dies first, the hardness vanishes away with his life. Men of excellent courage and audacity search out the holes where the dragons lie. Then watching until they come forth to feed, and passing by them with as

In the last half of the twentieth century, the years of the dragon in the Asian calendar were roughly equivalent to these years on the Western calendar: 1952, 1964, 1976, 1988, 2000.

much speed as they can, they cast them herbs to provoke sleep. So when the dragons are fast asleep, the men cut the stones out of their heads, and getting the booty of their heady enterprise, enjoy the reward of their rashness. The kings of the East wear these although they are so hard that no man can devise to imprint or engrave anything in it. It has a pure natural whiteness.'

In ancient legend, the blood of dragons was also magical. This fits with a fact noted on Dumbledore's *Famous Witches and Wizards* trading card, that one of his achievements was figuring out the twelve uses of dragon's blood.

See also:
Potter, Harry

Who Were the First British Wizards?

WIZARDS EXISTED IN BRITAIN LONG before Hogwarts was founded. Early wizards were known as Druids (as in Druidess Cliodna, who is depicted on a *Famous Witches and Wizards* trading card). The name comes from the Celtic for 'knowing the oak tree'. They were the scholarly class in Britain and Gaul (what is now France).

Druids acted as local priests, teachers, and judges. They also gathered annually in what is now the French city of Chartres to debate broader questions and settle controversies.

The Roman ruler Julius Caesar, who conquered Gaul and Britain and recorded what he learned of those lands, said the Druids 'discuss and teach to the youth many things respecting the stars and their motion, respecting the extent of the world and of our earth, respecting the nature of things, respecting the power and majesty of the immortal gods'.

For centuries scholars thought the Druids built Stonehenge, the circular monument on Salisbury Plain, England. But some now believe it is much older than Druid culture.

77

Druid training could last as long as twenty years. As Caesar suggests, it included instruction in poetry, astronomy, and philosophy, as well as religion.

The Druids worshipped several nature gods – they believed in a religious force that pervaded all living things. They also believed in immortality and reincarnation. Their rituals included animal and perhaps even human sacrifice. Caesar claimed they used twigs and branches to build huge frame sculptures in the shape of a man, then filled the inside of the sculptures with living people and set the sculptures ablaze. However, some scholars dispute this assertion, saying Caesar was unfairly biased against the Druids because they vigorously resisted his rule.

See also:
Death Eaters
Wizards

Why Doesn't Dumbledore Fight Voldemort?

OFFICIALLY, ALBUS DUMBLEDORE IS SIMPLY the headmaster of Hogwarts. But he is significantly more important in the magical world than such a role would imply. He is the only wizard, other than Harry, whom Voldemort fears – one of the few unafraid to speak of the fallen wizard by name. He had been first choice to lead the Ministry of Magic, but, preferring to remain at Hogwarts, he plays a behind-the-scenes role, advising Minister Cornelius Fudge.

Quite tall and thin, his hair and beard fall below his waist. He has a prominent, hawk-like nose, on which rest glasses with half-moon lenses. In Rowling's *Harry Potter and the Philosopher's Stone* his Chocolate Frog trading card says he is 'considered by many the greatest wizard of modern times', and he has the titles to prove it: Order of Merlin (First Class), Grand

Albus means 'white' in Latin. That befits a wizard with well-earned grey hair. It also makes him the perfect opponent of the 'Dark' Lord.

Sorcerer, Chief Warlock, Supreme Mugwump, International Confederation of Wizards.

A CLASSIC WIZARD

Dumbledore certainly is a wizard in the legendary mould. In appearance and dress, one might easily mistake him for Merlin of the Arthurian legends or Obi-Wan Kenobi of *Star Wars*. Gandalf, the wizard of J. R. R. Tolkien's *The Lord of the Rings* books, could be a twin brother, down to the fiery eyes that make one recall the scene in Rowling's *Harry Potter and the Goblet of Fire* when Dumbledore realizes Barty Crouch Jr has been fooling him: 'There was cold fury in every line of the ancient face; a sense of power radiated from Dumbledore as though he were giving off burning heat.'

'Dumbledore' is Old English word for bumblebee. J. K. Rowling says she liked the idea that this music-lover might hum to himself absent-mindedly.

WHY NOT SEARCH FOR VOLDEMORT?

Dumbledore, his trading card tells us, 'is particularly famous for his defeat of the dark wizard Grindelwald in 1945.' (*Harry Potter and the Philosopher's Stone* by J. K. Rowling) Since that was the same year that Britain and its allies defeated Hitler and other enemies of democracy in the Second World War, we can take it as a hint that Dumbledore and

Grindelwald had quite a struggle. So Dumbledore must be an accomplished fighter.

Why then would he let Harry face Voldemort? Surely he is powerful enough to find the Dark Lord and finish him once and for all?

A Child's Eyes

If only it were that easy. Dumbledore, for all his accomplishments and wisdom, is only human.

We usually see him as Harry would: all-knowing and all-powerful. He is the perfect parent – especially important to Harry, whose own parents are dead. To Harry, who knows only the version written in history books, Dumbledore's achievements seem too impressive to ever be matched. Meanwhile, Harry is full of doubts about his own abilities.

J. R. R. Tolkien, a noted scholar of Old English, named giant insects in *The Hobbit* 'Dumbledors'.

But, of course, Dumbledore is only human. What could one expect of a person who likes chamber music, tenpin bowling, and lemon drops? He must have had all the same doubts as Harry when he was young – maybe more. History books record only part of the story. (Trading cards even less.) We know he makes mistakes, like hiring Gilderoy Lockhart to teach Defence Against the Dark

Arts. Had Dumbledore been all-knowing, he would have seen through Lockhart. And of course in *Phoenix* he made the much greater mistake of not explaining to Harry exactly what was happening. But no one can be expected to know everything.

We can be certain Dumbledore has a plan for the defeat of Voldemort. But we also know he is patient. He may expect a one-on-one duel with the Dark Lord, regardless of any prophecy. Whether he is confident of winning such a battle or believes it will be just a prelude to a final conflict between Voldemort and Harry, is the sort of secret he is unlikely to reveal until the last moment. Whatever role he plays, in *Phoenix* Harry learned a crucial lesson on the road to becoming a mature wizard: He finally understood that Dumbledore is human, flawed like everyone else despite being deservedly revered. Now Harry can begin to see his own character and accomplishments as equally admirable.

See also:
Goblet of Fire
Hogwarts
Potter, Harry
Voldemort

Why Would Durmstrang Students Travel by Ship?

DURMSTRANG IS ONE OF TWO WIZARDING schools in continental Europe. Its exact location is a well-kept secret, but it is probably somewhere in northeastern Europe, judging from what J. K. Rowling tells us in *Harry Potter and the Goblet of Fire*: on top of robes of 'deep blood-red', the students wear coats of 'shaggy, matted fur'; and the Headmaster is named Igor Karkaroff.

'STORM AND STRESS'

The school's name is a play on the German phrase *Sturm und Drang* ('storm and stress'). That term describes a type of literature devoted to grandeur, spectacle, and rebellion. It was an important trend in German literature in the nineteenth century. The foremost writer of that movement was Johann Wolfgang von Goethe, whose most famous work, *Faust*,

Durmstrang is probably located close to the **Brocken**, a mountain in the Harz range in Germany where witches were said to run wild. (See **Death Eaters**.)

details a man's pact with the Devil – like the pact Karkaroff, a former Death Eater, made with Voldemort.

Another artist of the movement, composer Richard Wagner, wrote many dark operas, one of them based on the famous story of a ghost ship, *The Flying Dutchman*. That ship was doomed to roam the oceans endlessly because its captain had angrily denounced God during a storm. Rowling turned that ghost ship into a school bus.

PUREBRED EVIL

Durmstrang's name is more than a pun. It is a clue to the essential differences between it and Hogwarts. While Hogwarts students are taught only Defence Against the Dark Arts, students at Durmstrang are taught the Dark Arts themselves. (This is the influence of headmaster Karkaroff, a former Death Eater.) As well, Durmstrang 'does not admit Mudbloods', according to Draco Malfoy, whose father admires the Durmstrang doctrines and considered sending Draco there. This devotion to a nasty and highly questionable notion of purity befits the school's name. The artists of the *Sturm und Drang* movement, and Wagner in particular, were favourites of the Nazi government in

Sturm und Drang composer Richard Wagner also wrote a series of operas about a wizard named Alberic, who, like Harry, had an invisibility cloak. See **Wizards – Alberic Grunnion**.

Germany just before and during the Second World War. The Nazis were obsessed with killing anyone who did not fit their definition of a pure-blooded German.

EAST VERSUS WEST?

The differences between Hogwarts and Durmstrang also reflect long-standing animosity between countries of Western and Eastern Europe. Hogwarts, under Dumbledore's leadership, is a good example of the democratic

See also
Death Eaters

traditions of the West. Durmstrang is a more severe place, breeding wizards who can't be trusted – just as Eastern Europe has long been viewed by outsiders. Significantly, by the end of *Goblet*, both sides recognize that their enmity must be put aside to fight their common foe.

Where Does Magic Come From?

WHEN RON WEASLEY'S FAMILY MAKES A trip to Egypt in Rowling's *Harry Potter and the Prisoner of Azkaban*, Hermione admits, 'I'm really jealous. The ancient Egyptian wizards were fascinating.' Then in *Phoenix* she happily studies hieroglyphs, the pictures that Egyptians once used for a written language. She would probably agree with the many scholars who consider Egypt to be the origin of magical knowledge.

EGYPTIAN RELIGION AND MAGIC

Hieroglyphs record that Egyptian magic and religion were closely linked. The Egyptian gods, unlike those in other cultures, entrusted humans with magical wisdom. (By comparison, according to Greek mythology the hero Prometheus – whose name means 'to think ahead' – had to trick the gods into giving up fire, which represents life and knowledge.)

87

According to Egyptian religion, magic was created in the form of the god Heka soon after the creation of the world. Heka's name actually became the word that meant 'magic'. After that word was passed into Greek, where it was given a local spelling and pronunciation, it became the word *mageia*, which gives us the English word we use today.

Another Egyptian god, Thoth, was even more closely associated with magic. He ruled the healing arts – always linked with wizardry in ancient cultures – as well as astronomy and mathematics. He was often pictured carrying a pen, and was said to have written secret books

The Egyptian god **Thoth** recorded his magical knowledge in books.

that revealed the mysteries of alchemy and science. One of these books was supposedly sealed within a golden box that was kept within a hidden temple.

EGYPTIAN SPELLS

Egyptians relied heavily on charms and spells. Speaking of an action was said to make it so. Sometimes those words were spoken over a wax or clay figurine that represented the person or thing to which the magic was directed. These spells were commonly used for healing, but less benevolent uses were known. One wizard, Weba-aner, was said to have transfigured a small figurine of a crocodile into a live animal at court. The deadly beast killed the lover of the adulterous queen, then was returned to its original form by the wizard. Another wizard-priest became a ruler by using this technique to 'rule all kings by his magical power'. He sank figures of his enemies' fleets, causing the actual ships to sink.

The Egyptian god **Osiris** judged the dead.

However, Egyptian magic was less concerned with earthly riches than with holiness. According to one text, 'He who is a priest of the living . . . performs right actions without seeking a reward for them. Such a teacher lives a life of true piety.'

Egypt is also the origin of the scarab, a beetle that Hogwarts students know from Potions class.

Scarabs are called dung beetles because they gather and roll balls of dung in which

An Egyptian drawing of a **scarab** pushing the sun, with extended wings that signify the sun's rays.

they lay their eggs. In ancient Egypt this ball-rolling was seen to symbolize the movement of the sun. The scarab god Khepera was said to push the sun across the sky.

Eventually scarabs also came to symbolize immortality. Carved scarab amulets were placed on the heart of mummies to prepare them for their journey into the afterlife. Scarabs are still a common motif for jewellery.

See also:

Black, Sirius

Fawkes

Which Character Can't Die?

WHEN HARRY'S ADVENTURES BEGIN IN the first book, the oldest characters are Nicolas and Perenelle Flamel, who are both more than 600 years old. But they lose their immortality when the Philosopher's Stone is lost. However, another important character may be truly immortal: Fawkes, Dumbledore's pet phoenix.

The phoenix is a magical, eternal bird. It lives for centuries – some people say 500 years. The Latin poet Ovid said:

> There is a bird which renews itself again
> and again.
> The Assyrians gave this bird his name –
> the Phoenix.
> He does not live either on grain or herbs,
> but only on small drops of frankincense
> and juices of cardamom. When this bird

Because of its association with fire, the phoenix came to be a symbol of alchemists. That led to its appearance on the signs of chemists shops.

completes a full five centuries of life,
with his talons and with shining beak
he builds a nest high among the palm branches.
He places in this new nest
the cassia bark and ears of sweet spikenard
and some bruised cinnamon with yellow myrrh.
Then he lies among those dreamful scents,
and dies. And the Assyrians say
that from the body of the dying bird
is reproduced a little Phoenix which
is destined to live just as many years.

This sacred creature, almost always described as red and gold, was known as *benu* in ancient Egypt, where it originated. 'Phoenix' is actually a Greek word. It means both 'purple' and 'date palm tree', which leads scholars to guess that either the name came from a purple bird or from the idea that the phoenix built its nest at the top of a palm.

It was an important symbol of the city of Heliopolis ('Sun City'). In the Egyptian *Book of the Dead*, a religious text written about 2000 BC, the phoenix claims, 'I am the keeper of the Tablet of Destiny, the volume of the book of things which have happened and of things which shall be.' In Egyptian hieroglyphics, the phoenix image conveys the passage of time, and it remains a symbol of immortality today. Writers also use the phoenix to signify undying love and loyalty. In 'The Canonization', the seventeenth-century poet John Donne writes to his wife,

> *The phoenix riddle hath more wit*
> *By us; we two being one, are it.*
> *So, to one neutral thing both sexes fit,*
> *We die and rise the same, and prove*
> *Mysterious by this love.*

FAWKES'S NAME

Fawkes's name is related to the phoenix legend – but with a historical twist. Obviously he is named for Guy Fawkes, member of a famous attempt to blow up the English Parliament

In Asia, the phoenix is among the four mystical animals with great influence. The others are the dragon, the unicorn, and the tortoise.

building on 5 November 1605. The Gunpowder Plot, as it is called, was to be the start of a revolt by English Catholics, who were being persecuted at the time. The conspirators hid thirty-six barrels of gunpowder under the House of Lords, but there were so many conspirators that the plan leaked. Authorities arrested the men and executed many of them. (The situation for Catholics only became worse.) In Britain, 5 November is now Guy Fawkes Night, celebrated with bonfires – like the funeral pyre of a phoenix.

See also:

Black, Sirius

Egypt

Order of the

Phoenix

Was the Real Flamel a Successful Alchemist?

NICOLAS FLAMEL, AS MANY HARRY POTTER fans know, was an actual historical figure. Born near Paris about 1330, he tried several careers – poet, painter, and public scribe – before pursuing an interest in astrology. Then in 1357 he was visited in a dream by an angel who showed him a book and said, 'Flamel, look at this book. You will not in the least understand it, neither will anyone else; but the day will come when you will see in it something that no one else will see.' The next day he saw that same volume in a bookseller's stall, offered for a cheap price because no one could understand its writing. With great effort, and the help of a Spanish scholar who could read Hebrew, Flamel deciphered the text, which seemed to be a manual for changing common metals into gold.

Alchemists guarded their secrets with care, often using codes for their notes and letters.

Unfortunately, the instructions called for a special ingredient – a philosopher's stone – without describing it specifically. Flamel experimented for decades to find the mysterious substance, described only by pictures and symbols such dragons, griffins, a king leading soldiers, a rose bush and an oak tree.

On 17 January 1383, as he related in his memoir:

A building said to be the oldest existing house in Paris was built in 1407 by Nicolas Flamel. It is located at 51 rue de Montmorency.

Finally I found the object of my search, and I knew it by its strong smell; and with it I accomplished the magic. I had learned the preparation of the first agent and had only to follow my book word by word.

The first time I carried out the operation, I worked with quicksilver and transmuted about one and a half pounds of it into pure silver, better than silver from a mine. I put the results to the test several times. Later I accomplished the operation with the red stone on a similar amount of quicksilver on the 25th day of April of the same year when I transmuted the quick-silver into about the same amount of gold.

This gold was clearly superior to ordi-nary gold. I accomplished the magic three times with [my wife] Perenelle's help.

This description – 'its strong smell' – led other alchemists to believe the philosopher's stone was sulphur. But no one is known to have repeated the process.

Legends say that Flamel became rich with his discovery. There's certainly real proof of his wealth – almost too much proof. The real Flamel was very generous, paying for the building of hospitals, churches, and housing for the poor. Yet he left no sign of having mas-tered alchemical details. People have ransacked Flamel buildings many times since Flamel's death in 1417 but found nothing.

The truth, some scholars say, is that

Alchemists commonly worked with dangerous substances such as quicksilver (mercury), lead, arsenic, and strong acids. As a result they often suffered from strange illnesses.

Flamel's alchemy hobby may have been just a convenient cover for a less reputable source of wealth. It seems he actually became rich by lending money for a high fee. His supposed contact with Hebrew scholars in Spain is believed to have been a way to avoid admitting he did business with Jews there, because Jews were hated in France. Flamel would have faced the same resentment and anger if he hadn't discovered a way to hide the real reason he became rich.

Other legends say that in addition to creating gold Flamel produced the Elixir of Life, which offers immortality. Some of his followers said he and his wife actually lived on, sustained by the elixir. That fairy tale found its way into *Harry Potter and the Philosopher's Stone*. At the beginning the story Flamel and his wife are both alive and well, despite being just shy of 660 years old. Unfortunately, when the Philosopher's Stone is destroyed their elixir can no longer be produced, so they pass away.

See also:
Alchemy
Voldemort
Wizards

Why Would Fluffy Come From 'a Greek Chappie'?

FLUFFY IS HAGRID'S PET DOG, GUARDIAN OF the Philosopher's Stone after it is removed from Gringotts Bank: Rowling describes him in *Harry Potter and the Philosopher's Stone* as 'a monstrous dog, a dog that filled the whole space between ceiling and floor. It had three heads; three pairs of rolling, mad eyes; three noses, twitching and quivering in their direction; three drooling mouths.'

J. K. Rowling says that Hagrid bought Fluffy from 'a Greek chappie I met in the pub.' That makes sense, because Fluffy is actually a magical creature from Greek mythology known as Cerberus. He was a sentry there too. He guarded Hades, the underworld, where the souls of the dead go to live for eternity. It was his job to keep all living beings away, and to eat anyone trying to escape.

According to some legends **Cerberus** had a hundred heads, and in others snakes also grew from his necks.

CERBERUS AND HERCULES

Cerberus plays a role in a famous Greek myth, the story of the twelve labours of Hercules. The hero Hercules had been tricked by the goddess Hera into committing horrendous crimes, and was punished by becoming a servant to an unworthy king for twelve years. The king demanded that Hercules complete twelve tasks considered impossible. Most of them involved killing or capturing vicious beasts, like the Hydra, a creature with many heads. The last, considered the most difficult, was to capture Cerberus from his post at the gates of Hades and parade him before the king. Amazingly, Hercules did so, using just brute strength.

See also:
Centaurs
Sphinx

CERBERUS AND MUSIC

One other person got the better of Cerberus, but it wasn't with muscle. Orpheus, a gifted musician, braved the underworld to rescue his beloved, Eurydice. Lacking the strength of Hercules, he played his lyre to tame Cerberus. It worked. He was able to sneak by the creature, and to escort Eurydice away. That's why the Greek chappie told Hagrid music is the way to tame Fluffy.

Cerberus, from an illustration drawn about AD 1500.

Why Would the Forest Near Hogwarts Be 'Forbidden'?

FORESTS ARE A FAVOURITE CREATION OF writers, and J. K. Rowling's Forbidden Forest near Hogwarts has all the qualities one could expect. It is nature run wild, making it the opposite of civilized places like Hogwarts or the village of Hogsmeade. Within it live magical creatures older than humankind, like the unicorn. As well, just as there is knowledge

in nature that humans have always tried to understand – such as the wisdom of the nature gods worshipped by the Druids – the Forbidden Forest near Hogwarts is a place where secrets are kept and mysteries can be unravelled. Voldemort's murder of a unicorn in *Stone* reveals his presence to Harry; in *Chamber*, Harry and Ron follow spiders into the Forest and meet Aragog, who tells them a little about the monster in Hogwarts.

As with other forests in literature, Rowling's Forbidden Forest is also a dangerous place where one can lose one's way or one's sense of self. But forests can also offer refuge, and are home to spirits with a special knowledge of nature and healing. Hagrid, for instance, does not fear the Forbidden Forest. And if Harry ever needed to escape Voldemort, he could easily find himself protected by the Forbidden Forest and its residents, rather than endangered by them.

See also:
Centaurs
Druids
Hogwarts
Unicorns

What Does Ice Cream Have to Do With Witchcraft?

IN *AZKABAN*, FLOREAN FORTESCUE HELPS Harry by telling him about witch burnings, and in *Phoenix* he complains loudly that the Ministry of Magic has made a deal with criminals. Why does this ice-cream shop owner know so much about witchcraft law?

The answer lies in his family name. The Fortescues are well known in English history. The career of one of member of the family, Sir John Fortescue (c. 1531-1607), ranged from tutoring Princess Elizabeth (the future Elizabeth I) to serving as her Chancellor of the Exchequer when she was Queen. In between, it was his job to enforce the tough witchcraft laws that Elizabeth's Parliament passed in 1563. He led the first important trials under those laws, apparently with the same severe attitude Florean Fortescue expresses. In one trial, a woman was executed on charges that included receiving instructions from a talking cat.

Other members of the Fortescue family include one of the most influential legal minds in British history, and a saint.

Some people
say Elizabeth I's
laws against
witches were
harsh to prove
that she was
not one herself.
Her mother,
Anne Boleyn,
had been
executed on
witchcraft
charges by order
of Elizabeth's
father,
Henry VIII.
Sir John
Fortescue was
also a close
relative of Anne
Boleyn.

So what about the name 'Florean'? That may be an inside joke. You'll recall that Harry gets to know Florean Fortescue when he spends a lot of time writing his essays at the ice-cream shop. That should bring to mind J. K. Rowling, well known for having planned and written so much of Harry's story in a café. As she has said, 'My ideal writing space is a large café with a small corner table near a window overlooking an interesting street (for gazing out of in search of inspiration). It would serve very strong coffee . . .' Since 1720, writers who feel the same way, including Lord Byron, Goethe, Charles Dickens and Marcel Proust have worked at the tables of a particular coffee shop, making it the most famous in Europe. For inspiration they've looked out on Venice's adored St Mark's Square. And their very strong coffee has come in cups decorated with the shop's name: Caffè Florian.

Are All Giants All Bad?

G IANTS ARE THOUGHT BY MOST HUMANS – probably unfairly – to be as dangerous and cruel as they are large. But there's no denying they can be difficult, as Hagrid learns in *Phoenix* when he meets Grawp, Karkus, and Golgomath. Whatever the truth, they have a troublesome history.

EARLY GIANTS

The first giants were the Gigantes of ancient Greek mythology, born when the blood of Uranus (the Heavens) fell upon Gaea (Earth). The Gigantes fought the gods of Mount Olympus – Zeus, Hera, Apollo and others. The Olympian gods needed the help of the hero Hercules to defeat them. The Gigantes were buried underneath mountains that then became volcanoes.

The **Cyclops** of Greek myth.

Another race of mythical Greek giants was known as the Cyclops. These monsters, who

In two early books of the Bible, Genesis and Ezekiel, **Magog** is the name of the place from which **Gog** comes. In a later book, Revelation, Magog is a second creature or force who joins Gog in trying to destroy the world.

Perhaps **Golgomath** in *Phoenix* is a descendant of Gogmagog and another well-known biblical giant, Goliath of Gath.

had only one eye, created the thunderbolts of Zeus. In Homer's epic poem *The Odyssey*, the hero Odysseus and his men encounter a Cyclops and barely escape.

Both these races of giants, like those that followed, were said to be vicious cannibals.

BRITISH GIANTS

Among later giants, the legend of a pair named Gog and Magog spread throughout the world, changing a bit from place to place. In Britain the story survives in the form of two large statues in Guildhall in London, first erected in the 1400s and said to portray the last of a race of giants destroyed by the legendary founder of London. (The statues, public favourites, have been replaced twice: first after the Great Fire of 1666, then after an air raid during the Second World War.)

A slightly different British legend combines those giants into a single monster named Gogmagog, who lived near Cornwall. In that version, a brave soldier threw the giant off a cliff, which is still called Giant's Leap.

Another British giant of legend, Gargantua, became famous in the 1500s as the main character in comical adventures written by a Frenchman, François Rabelais. Gargantua was something like the gigantic American woodsman Paul Bunyan. He was so huge that a tennis court could fit inside one of his teeth. It took the milk of 17,913 cows to quench his thirst.

GIANTS AND MAGIC

According to the early historian Geoffrey of Monmouth, Stonehenge, the mysterious circle of huge stones in southern England, originated with the giants of Ireland. As he records, Merlin had been asked for advice on building a war memorial. The wizard replied:

'If you want to grace the burial place of these men with some lasting monument, send for the Giants' Ring which is on Mount Killaraus in Ireland. In that place there is a stone construction which no man of this period could ever erect, unless he combined great skill and artistry. The stones are enormous and there is no one alive strong enough to move them. If they are placed in position round this site, in the way in which they are erected over there, they will stand for ever . . .

'These stones are connected with secret religious rites and they have various properties which are medicinally important. Many years ago the Giants transported

In William Shakespeare's *As You Like It*, Rosalind anxiously asks her friend Celia about a young man: 'What said he? How looked he? Where went he? Did he ask for me? Where remains he? How parted with thee? And when shalt thou see him again? Answer me in one word.'
Celia snaps back, 'You must borrow me **Gargantua's** mouth first; 'tis a word too great for any mouth of this age's size.' (Act III, scene ii)

them from the remotest confines of Africa and set them up in Ireland at a time when they inhabited that country. Their plan was that, whenever they felt ill, baths should be prepared at the foot of the stones; for they used to pour water over them and to run this water into baths in which their sick were cured. What is more, they mixed the water with herbal concoctions and so healed their wounds. There is not a single stone among them that hasn't some medicinal virtue.'

Geoffrey of Monmouth, like most early historians, relied on stories he was told, so his history of Britain mixes legends with actual events.

As Geoffrey tells it, the king took Merlin's advice and had the stones transported to their present site.

A SECRET EVERYONE KNOWS

In Harry's world, most wizards are prejudiced against giants. Hagrid never told anyone his mother was the giantess Fridwulfa because he was worried about what they would think. For the same reason, the headmistress of Beauxbatons, Madame Olympe Maxime, is reluctant to admit she is also half-giant. But anyone with common sense would guess that secret from her name. Olympe refers to the original giants of Olympus, and *maxime* means 'great' or 'very large' in French.

Which Real-Life Creature Still Eludes Scientists?

Giant Squid

IN THE LAKE AT HOGWARTS LIVES A REAL-LIFE creature that is as mysterious as any magical beast. It is not elusive because it is small; in fact, it is the largest invertebrate on earth. It is the giant squid, which lives in waters so deep and far from shore that no human living today has seen one alive.

Architeuthis, as scientists call it, can grow to seventy feet long. Its eyes, the largest of any animal, are well-suited for gathering what little light exists in the mile-deep waters of its home. There is no sunlight at those depths, but certain creatures have chemicals in their bodies that glow.

The French science fiction author Jules Verne wrote about the giant squid in his novel *20,000 Leagues*

Under the Sea. The creature attacks the electric submarine in the story, *Nautilus*:

> Before my eyes was a horrible monster, worthy to figure in the legends of the marvellous. It was an immense cuttlefish, being eight yards long. It swam crossways in the direction of the *Nautilus* with great speed, watching us with its enormous staring green eyes. Its eight arms, or rather feet, fixed to its head, that have given the name of cephalopod to these animals, were twice as long as its body, and were twisted like the Furies' hair. One could see the 250 air-holes on the inner side of the tentacles. The monster's mouth, a horned beak like a parrot's, opened and shut vertically. Its tongue, a horned substance, furnished with several rows of pointed teeth, came out quivering from this veritable pair of shears.

Verne was following a long tradition in making the giant squid out to be a villain. But, turning our expectations about monsters upside down as usual, J. K. Rowling's giant squid is kind. When Dennis Creevey falls into the lake in *Goblet*, the squid rescues him, placing him back into the boat.

Sailors called the giant squid the **Kraken**. Many people believed the exaggerated reports that the Kraken was two kilometres wide and looked like an island when it surfaced.

Why Are Harry and Cedric Like Knights of the Round Table?

THE GOBLET OF FIRE IS A 'ROUGHLY HEWN wooden cup' that would be 'entirely unremarkable had it not been full to the brim with dancing blue-white flames', writes Rowling in *Harry Potter and the Goblet of Fire*. By magic, it calls on certain wizards to test their skills in the Triwizard Tournament. That challenge and its mysterious source link the competitors, including Harry and Cedric Diggory, to the legends of King Arthur and the Round Table.

The Goblet of Fire is more than a little similar to another powerful goblet that has launched tournaments and battles: the Holy Grail. This is the cup from which Jesus Christ drank at the Last Supper. Though sometimes depicted as a shining silver goblet, the Holy Grail, being the cup of a poor carpenter, would probably have been made of wood – like the Goblet of Fire. The Grail is also a magical object. To drink from it is to be miraculously healed. And like the Goblet, it can sense whether or not a person is worthy.

According to legend, King Arthur, praying for a sign from heaven during a barren period in his reign, sees the Grail. (In the earliest stories the Grail was a large platter; over time it became a cup.) He and his knights then undertook quests to either capture it or at least understand its significance.

In Harry's world the final task of the Triwizard Tournament is also to literally find a Grail, in this case the Triwizard Cup, and to win it for Hogwarts. And just as the Grail in Arthurian legend is found by Galahad, son of Lancelot, because his soul is completely pure, Harry and Cedric Diggory succeed in reaching the Cup through strength of character as much as wizarding skill.

One of Dumbledore's middle names, '**Percival**', connects him to the Grail. Most of the legends focus on a young peasant named Perceval who proves his virtue and becomes a great Knight of the Round Table.

See also:
Mazes
Potter, Harry

Why Are Goblins Such Good Bankers?

NOT NEARLY AS FRIENDLY AS ELVES, AND more clever than gnomes, the goblins of Harry's world have rebelled against wizards several times in the past. The truce between the two sides is uneasy, and the wizard world has not yet embraced goblins.

THE GOOD, THE BAD, AND THE UGLY

The word *goblin* derives from the Greek *kobalos*, meaning 'rogue'. The same word produced the German *kobold* or *kobolt* and the French *gobelin*. As 'rogue' suggests, goblins tend not to haunt a single family or home but rather are given to roam.

Sometimes goblins are portrayed as more industrious than evil – adept at mining and metalwork, for example. Their cousins, the hobgoblins, also tended to be more pranksters than malefactors. Puck, 'that merry wanderer of the night' from Shakespeare's *A Midsummer Night's Dream*, is the best example.

They have even been known to do good deeds. Long before he wrote *A Christmas Carol*, Charles Dickens wrote 'The Story of the Goblins Who Stole a Sexton', a Christmas story in which goblins showed a man named Gabriel Grub — 'an ill-conditioned, cross-grained, surly fellow; a morose and lonely man, who consorted with nobody but himself' — the error of his ways:

Seated on an upright tombstone, close to him, was a strange, unearthly figure, whom Gabriel felt at once was no being of this world. His long, fantastic legs which might have reached the ground, were cocked up, and crossed after a quaint, fantastic fashion; his sinewy arms were bare; and his hands rested on his knees. On his short, round body, he wore a close covering, ornamented with small slashes; a short cloak dangled at his back; the collar was cut into curious peaks, which served the goblin in lieu of ruff or neckerchief; and his shoes curled up at his toes into long points. On his head, he wore a broad-brimmed sugar-loaf hat, garnished with a single feather. The hat

People used to rid themselves of goblins by spreading **flax** seeds on their kitchen floor. For some reason, the goblin was compelled to pick up all the seeds – a very boring task. The goblin would soon look for fun elsewhere.

was covered with white frost; and the goblin looked as if he had sat on the same tombstone very comfortably, for two or three hundred years. He was sitting perfectly still; his tongue was put out, as if in derision; and he was grinning at Gabriel Grub with such a grin as only a goblin could call up.

'I am afraid my friends want you, Gabriel,' said the goblin, thrusting his tongue farther into his cheek than ever – and a most astonishing tongue it was – 'I'm afraid my friends want you, Gabriel,' said the goblin.

Like the ghosts in *A Christmas Carol* who show Scrooge the meaning of Christmas, the goblins show Gabriel that the world isn't as bad as it seems.

However, goblins are most often portrayed like those of Christina Rosetti's poem, 'Goblin Market':

We must not look at goblin men,
We must not buy their fruits:
Who knows upon what soil they fed
Their hungry thirsty roots? . . .
Their offers should not charm us,
Their evil gifts would harm us.

Magical creature expert Carol Rose says some goblins are known to be nice to children even if they don't like adults.

J. R. R. Tolkien introduced bad goblins in *The Hobbit* and then made them truly wicked in *The Lord of the Rings*, for which he changed their name to 'Orcs'. In his invented history of Middle-earth the Orcs were bred from tortured elves, the creatures Tolkein loved, and became the Elves' opposites. As Tolkien scholar Robert Foster says, 'They hated all things of beauty, and loved to kill and destroy.' The Orcs become the army of Tolkien's Dark Lord.

J. K. Rowling's goblins seem to be somewhere between good and evil. That balance makes them perfect guardians for Gringotts Bank, a task that requires they be both trustworthy and ruthless.

See also:
Boggarts
Cornish Pixies
Trolls
Veela

Which of Draco's Sidekicks Is Also Named for a Dragon?

JUST AS DRACO'S NAME COMES FROM THE Latin word for dragon, 'Gregory Goyle' echoes 'gargoyle', the monster seen near the roofs of some buildings. Less well-known is the source of that creature's name: the Gargouille, a serpent-like dragon from France.

The Gargouille lived in the Seine River. It spouted water with great force, overturning fishing boats and flooding the country-side. St Romain, the Archbishop of Rouen, used a convict as bait to lure the monster from the river, then made the sign of the cross to sub-due the beast. He walked it

117

See also:

Malfoy

Names

to the city, where the residents slaughtered it.

Eventually, craftsmen carved images of the creature on the waterspouts they built to direct rainwater away from the walls of buildings.

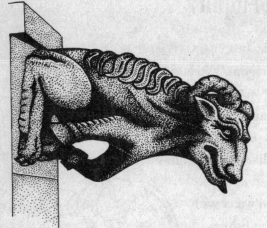

Which Creature Is Master of Both Earth and Sky?

Harry's Hogwarts house, Gryffindor, literally means 'golden griffin' in French. (*Or* is French for 'gold'.) It's an appropriate name for a house characterized by courage and virtue.

Griffins (sometimes spelled 'gryphons') are magical creatures, part lion, part eagle. They originated in India, where they guarded huge treasures of gold. In the third century AD a historian named Aelian wrote:

> I have heard that the Indian animal the Gryphon is a quadruped like a lion; that it has claws of enormous strength and that they resemble those of a lion. Men commonly report that it is winged and that the feathers along its back are black, and those on its front are red, while the actual wings are neither but are white.

Griffin, from the seal of an Austrian town, about 1315.

119

And Ctesias [an ancient Greek historian] records that its neck is variegated with feathers of a dark blue; that it has a beak like an eagle's, and a head too, just as artists portray it in pictures and sculpture. Its eyes, he says, are like fire.

It builds its lair among the mountains. Although it is not possible to capture the full-grown animal, hunters do take the young ones. Gryphons engage too with other beasts and overcome them without difficulty, but they will not face the lion or the elephant.

In *Alice in Wonderland*, Alice meets the Gryphon, who is anything but fierce. He and the Mock Turtle tell Alice about their old school days and teach her an unusual dance, the Lobster Quadrille.

THE MEANING OF GRIFFINS

Griffins have been part of literature and mythology for dozens of centuries. In that time, their symbolic meaning has changed greatly. Scholar Hans Biedermann explains:

A fabulous animal, symbolically significant for its domination of both the earth and the sky because of its lion's body and eagle's head and wings. In Greece the griffin was a symbol of vigilant strength; Apollo rode one, and griffins guarded the gold of Hyperborea [a mythical land of perpetual sunshine and happiness 'beyond the north wind']. The griffin was also an embodiment of Nemesis, the goddess of retribution, and turned her wheel of fortune. In legend the creature was a symbol of *superbia* (arrogant pride), because Alexander the Great was said to have tried to fly on the backs of griffins to the edge of the sky.

At first also portrayed as a satanic figure entrapping human souls, the creature later became a symbol of the dual nature (divine and human) of Jesus Christ, precisely because of its mastery of earth and sky. The solar associations of both the lion

In *Paradise Lost*, John Milton refers to the griffins' continuous struggle against a tribe of thieves:
'As when a
  gryphon,
  through the
  wilderness . . .
Pursues the
  Arimaspian,
  who by stealth
Had from his
  wakeful
  custody
  purloined
The guarded
  gold.'
(Book II, 943-6)

and the eagle favoured this positive read-ing. The griffin thus also became the adversary of serpents and basilisks, both of which were seen as embodiments of satanic demons.

See also:

Beasts

Hippogriffs

For the last thousand years, the griffin has been a favourite on family crests. An expert in heraldry says, 'The griffin is very popular, for it has numerous virtues and apparently no vices. Notable among the former are vigilance, courage and strength.' These are the very qual-ities embodied in the founder of Hogwarts whose name comes from this creature, Godric Gryffindor, and of the members of Gryffindor House.

Why Do Parents Worry About Grindylows?

GRINDYLOWS ARE WATER DEMONS FROM the legends of Yorkshire. J. K. Rowling introduces them in *Harry Potter and the Prisoner of Azkaban*: 'A sickly green creature with sharp little horns had its face pressed against the glass, pulling faces and flexing its long, spindly fingers.'

These dangerous creatures have a fondness for ponds and lakes, where unsuspecting children who get too close to the water's edge can be caught and dragged under the surface. In Lancashire, the same demon is known as Jenny Greenteeth. In other parts of England it is known as Nellie Long-Arms. A relative of the grindylow, Peg o' the Well, haunts wells.

Carol Rose, an expert on demons and spirits, calls grindylows 'nursery bogies, described with vigour by watchful nursemaids and anxious parents in order to prevent the

Every culture and every era has its water bogeys. This is from a medieval woodcut.

See also:

Giant Squid

Kappas

Merpeople

untimely death of children in such fearful places.' But when Harry dives into the Hogwarts lake to rescue Ron during the second task of the Triwizard Tournament, the grindylows who grab his leg and robes feel very real to him.

Where Do The Nastiest Mandrakes Grow?

STRANGE BUT TRUE: IN EARLY VERSIONS OF the Cinderella fairy tale, the heroine was helped by a hazel tree rather than a fairy godmother. Once upon a time that would have been common. No doubt it goes back to the first stories ever told. Nature spirits and tree gods appear in mythology and every ancient religion, and in fact trees were still the focus of some sacred rituals in Europe a thousand years after Christianity began.

In botany as in the rest of her wizarding world, J. K. Rowling brings together past and present.

Plants are also the inspiration for the names of many of Rowling's characters, including Harry's mother, Lily, and his Aunt Petunia. (See **Names**)

A ROSE BY ANOTHER NAME . . .

Because plants have always been given strange names it can be difficult to guess which plants in the stories are taken from real life and which are imaginary. Any plant dictionary will have names worthy of Rowling's wordplay: Viper's Bugloss, Stinking Gladwin, Hercules' All-Heal, Rupture-Wort, Mugwort, Saracen's Confound, Flea-Wort, Serpent's Tongue, Alehoof, Colewort, Bishop's-Weed, Butter-Bur, Mouse-Ear, Coralwort, Throat-Wort, Stinking Arrach, Loosestrife, Ramping Fumitory, Miltwaste, Hare's Ear Treacle. Yes, all of those are real plants. Some are common-place. The names come from a famous book that Rowling has acknowledged as a source, *The Complete Herbal* by Nicholas Culpeper (1616–1654). 'I used to collect names of plants that sounded witchy', she told an interviewer, 'and then I found this and it was the answer to my every prayer.'

Among the real plants Rowling uses in the novels are belladonna, wolfsbane, knotgrass, wormwood, hellebore, and daisies. Those are used in Snape's Potions class, so they are described in detail in the chapter on Potions that follows. It's enough to say here that, as you have come to expect, Rowling makes sure her wizards use them as herbalists have done for centuries.

Gillyweed, which Harry uses during the Triwizard Tournament, is a joke on a real plant nickname, 'gillyflower', given to both the carnation and a wallflower. The name comes from a mispronunciation of an old French word; but Rowling's invention fulfills the name's promise. It actually gives a person gills.

Dittany, another real plant, is mentioned in *Stone*. Although Harry is distracted before he learns about it, one type of dittany from the island of Crete has been long thought to have magical powers. It was even mentioned in Virgil's epic *The Aeneid*. In that story the goddess Venus, looking on a battlefield, is

> . . . *mov'd with grief,*
> *And pierc'd with pity, hastens her relief.*
> *A branch of healing dittany she brought,*
> *Which in the Cretan fields with care she*
>   *sought . . .*
> *This Venus brings, in clouds involv'd, and*
>   *brews*
> *Th' extracted liquor with ambrosian dews,*
> *And odorous panacee* [panacea, or cure-all].
> (Bk. XII, 608–617)

HUSH, LITTLE BABY

The Mandrake, or mandragora, which Professor Sprout introduces in the second year, seems far too strange to be connected to legend. It's hard to imagine it could be anything but a Rowling invention. How could anyone really believe a plant was a small,

Dragon Blood: Calamus

Dragon Scales: Bistort

Five Fingers: Cinquefoil

Hawk's Heart: Wormwood seed

Lamb's Ears: Betony

Lion's Hair: Turnip leaves

Nose Bleed: Yarrow

Pig's Tail: Leopard's Bane

Skin of Man: Fern

Swine's Snout: Dandelion leaves

Wolf Foot: Bugle Weed

screaming human? But that's exactly what many people thought. Because the root of the plant is shaped vaguely like a human, the plant was thought to contain a human spirit, to feel pain, and to bleed and scream when pulled from the ground. Uprooting it, or hearing the scream, could kill a person. However, once in hand, the plant could be worn as a powerful amulet.

An accurate drawing of a **mandrake** root and a medieval woodcut illustrating the fanciful version.

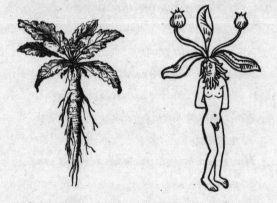

Each plant supposedly could be identified as either male or female, so in time the mandrake became associated with love and fertility. It was often used in medicine to ease pain, and scientists now know it contains a strong narcotic that can work well in low doses or be fatal if too much is taken. Lazy men were said to have 'eaten mandrake'. In Shakespeare's *Antony and Cleopatra*, Cleopatra demands, 'Give me to drink mandragora . . . that I might sleep out this great gap of time my Antony is away' (Act I, scene v). As a love potion, too, it was important to avoid drinking too much. A little bit might work, but a lot would make the lover act like a fool. Yet it must have been effective: Venus, known as the goddess of love, was sometimes called Mandragoritis.

Because mandrakes were said to contain spirits, they were sometimes asked questions as if they were fortunetellers. The roots supposedly nodded or shook their heads in reply. The human shape also led to mandrakes being used like voodoo dolls: a spell or curse might be placed on the root in order to have an effect on a real person. This sort of magic was eventually outlawed and the mandrake came to be considered evil. In some places it was said that mandrakes grew from the blood that dripped from hanged criminals.

In *Chamber*, Hermione explains to the class that the mandrake can restore people who have been somehow changed from their usual selves. That also fits with legend. One of the most famous transformations in legend involved mandrakes. In Homer's epic *The Odyssey*, mandrakes helped the sorcerer Circe change Odysseus's men into pigs and then back into humans again.

Had Harry finished studying about **dittany** instead of being distracted by Hagrid's sudden interest in baby dragons in *Stone*, he might also have discovered another kind of real dittany that, although less useful, is spectacular enough to impress the Weasley twins. It is covered in a resin that gives off a vapour that bursts into flame when lit. (The plant itself is left unhurt.)

See also:
Names
Potions

It's fairly obvious that Harry and Ron should pay more attention in Herbology. There's more to the subject than gardening. Many of Professor Sprout's plants are as interesting as the creatures they meet in Hagrid's class. And like Hagrid's magical creatures, some come from legend and real life. Sadly, it seems that whenever Harry has to read an old book about plants his mind wanders or he falls asleep. That doesn't seem to be a problem for J. K. Rowling.

Which Is the Least Likely Magical Creature?

Buckbeak the hippogriff, introduced in *Azkaban*, is more than just an unusual magical creature. With the bird-like head and forelegs of a griffin attached to the body of a horse, hippogriffs are an especially odd combination. That's just what was intended by the man who imagined them, a sixteenth-century author with sense of humour.

The Roman poet Virgil once described something as impossible by saying it would only happen when 'griffins are mated with horses'. The phrase stuck. For centuries it was used just as someone today might say, 'When pigs have wings.' Ludovico Ariosto, an Italian court poet of the early 1500s, remembered that line when he was writing *Orlando Furioso*, an epic story about the knights of Charlemagne, a king who ruled much of Europe in the ninth century. Deciding the time had come to make

Ludovico Ariosto
(1474–1533)

Virgil's unlikely match, he created the hippogriff. (The Greek word for horse is *hippos*.)

According to Ariosto, the hippogriff comes from the Rhiphaean Mountains, 'far beyond the icebound seas.' The creature appears in the story when Charlemagne's brave niece, Bradamante, searches for her beloved, a knight named Rogero. Bradamante discovers Rogero is the captive of an enchanter who rides the strange creature, which few people have seen before. After defeating the enchanter and freeing Rogero, Bradamante approaches the beast:

In Ariosto's version of the story, the brave knights Bradamante and Rogero are said to be ancestors of the family that employed Ariosto while he wrote the epic. Not true to life, but a polite gesture.

> They descended from the mountain to the spot where the encounter had taken place. There they found the Hippogriff, with the magic buckler in its wrapper, hanging to his saddle-bow. Bradamante advanced to seize the bridle; the Hippogriff seemed to wait her approach, but before she reached him he spread his wings and flew away to a neighbouring hill, and in the same manner, a second time, eluded her efforts.
>
> Rogero and the other liberated knights dispersed over the plain and hill-tops to secure him, and at last the animal allowed Rogero to seize his rein. The fearless Rogero hesitated not to vault upon his

back, and let him feel his spurs, which so roused his mettle that, after galloping a short distance, he suddenly spread his wings, and soared into the air.

Bradamante had the grief to see her lover snatched away from her at the very moment of reunion. Rogero, who knew not the art of directing the horse, was unable to control his flight. He found himself carried over the tops of the mountains, so far above them that he could hardly distinguish what was land and what water.

The Hippogriff directed his flight to the west, and cleaved the air as swiftly as

The name **'Charlemagne'** comes from combining the title 'Charles Magnus', meaning Charles the Great.

The tales of
Charlemagne
and his twelve
Paladins – the
peers of his
court – are as
widespread as
the Celtic tales
of King Arthur
and the Knights
of the Round
Table. The
knight Orlando
(known as
Roland in some
versions) is
usually the
greatest hero.

a new-rigged vessel cut the waves, impelled by the freshest and most favourable gales.

In another episode of the story, a different knight, Astolfo, rides the same hippogriff across the world:

Hawk and eagle soar a course less free. Over the wide land of Gaul the warrior flew, from Pyrenees to Rhine, from sea to sea. To Aragon he passed out of Navarre, leaving people below wondering at the sight, then crossed Castile, Gallicia, Lisbon, Seville and Cordova. He left no coast or inland plain of Spain unexplored.

From the Atlantic to the farther side of Egypt, bent over Africa, he turned. Morocco, Fez and Oran, looking down, noble Biserta next and Tunis-town. Tripoli, Berniche, Ptolomitta he viewed, and into Asia's land the Nile he pursued.

Eventually Astolfo rides the hippogriff all the way to Paradise. Later, he respectfully sets it free. One can understand why J. K. Rowling says in *Beasts* that the hippogriff 'is now found worldwide'.

See also:
Beasts
Griffins

Why Would Anyone Go to School with a Slytherin?

T HE WRITER PICO IYER, WHO ATTENDED two of Britain's older boarding schools, the Dragon School and Eton, says 'much in the Harry Potter universe can seem familiar':

Here are all the rites I remember as vividly as lemon drops: the cryptic list of instructions that would appear through the mail, describing what we must – and mustn't – bring to school (the point of all the rules being not to make order so much as to enforce obedience); the trip to dusty old shops with creaky family names – New & Lingwood or Alden & Blackwell – where aged men would fit us out with the approved uniform and equipment, as they had done for our fathers and our fathers' fathers; the special school train that would be waiting in a London station to transport us to our

Hogwarts is located in **Scotland**. Its appearance is not modelled on a real building, says J. K. Rowling. The design comes from her imagination.

cells. Once the doors clanged shut behind us, we knew we were inside an alternative reality where none of the usual rules applied . . .

One could even say that the stranger the detail in Rowling's world, the closer it is to something everyday to us as gruel. Harry plays Quidditch, a peculiar game featuring 'Bludgers' and 'Chasers' and 'Quaffles'; we had three brutal sports not played in any other school, the most savage of which had 'walls' and 'behinds' and no official goal scored since 1909. At Harry's school, inscrutably, 'the third-floor corridor on the right-hand side is out of bounds'; at Eton, we were not allowed to walk on one side of the main road through town (for reasons that were not forthcoming). As for ghosts, we ate and slept and studied around busts and portraits and the scribbled desktop signatures of [the British prime ministers] Gladstone, Wellington and Pitt the Elder.

But some people say that Hogwarts is quite different from most boarding schools. It is pleasant: the food is delicious and Harry sleeps in a four-poster bed. It is lenient: though disobedience may cost a few house points, the

It's fitting that Harry begins each school year with a ride on the **Hogwarts Express**. J. K. Rowling thought up the stories during a train ride.

teachers are very forgiving. Most of all, Dumbledore has made it a place of eminent fairness.

Given how agreeable the school can be, one has to wonder what the Slytherins are doing there. Every bit of trouble seems to start with a Slytherin. There doesn't seem to be a decent student in that house. Its philosophy seems to be the same dark thought expressed by Quirrell in Rowling's *Harry Potter and the Philosopher's Stone*: 'There is no good and evil, there is only power, and those too weak to seek it.' Salazar Slytherin, the Hogwarts founder for whom the house was named, was so devious he even built the Chamber of Secrets under the school without telling the

J. K. Rowling has a soft spot for **King's Cross** station in London, where the Hogwarts Express stops, because that is where her mother and father met.

other founders. So wouldn't it make sense to just get rid of them?

Actually, that would seem to be the opposite of J. K. Rowling's philosophy. In fact, the presence of Slytherins at Hogwarts seems to say a lot about her ideas of good and evil.

Within the walls of Hogwarts, Dumbledore has created an appealing ideal. Evil is not pushed away fearfully; or simply met with force. It is to be countered with compassion. More than once, Dumbledore has demonstrated a strong faith that fallen wizards can redeem themselves.

Each of the four founders of Hogwarts had individual qualities that form part of a balanced whole. Even Slytherin's ambition can be directed towards good – provided it is balanced with the characteristics displayed by the others. It is part of reality, part of every individual – just as Harry has a bit of Voldemort in him. Trying to eliminate it would be silly, as well as impossible.

See also:
Durmstrang
Names

For the many teachers and students who fail to understand the role Hogwarts plays in bringing those qualities together, the Sorting Hat's new song in *Phoenix* – which expresses concern about splitting the students in the first place – sends a clear message: don't let small differences divide you.

Which Creature May Not Bow Its Head?

H ARRY LEARNS ABOUT KAPPAS, 'CREEPY, water-dwellers that looked like scaly monkeys', in Rowling's *Harry Potter and the Prisoner of Azkaban*. They are mentioned again in *Beasts*.

J. K. Rowling did not invent kappas. They are, as she says in *Beasts*, water demons of Japanese legend. (In *Harry Potter and the Prisoner of Azkaban*, Professor Snape makes an error when he informs Harry's class that 'the kappa is more commonly found in Mongolia'.) Like the grindylows who live near Hogwarts, kappas live in lakes and rivers, and capture people in the water. They are also known as Kawako, which means 'Child of the River'.

The description in *Beasts*, odd as it sounds, is true to legend. Kappas can be vicious and enjoy the taste of blood.

However, a human may escape from a kappa by exploiting the creature's greatest weakness. Its vitality is drawn from a saucer-like depression on its head, which must remain filled with water. If one offers a polite and ceremonious bow, the kappa will be obligated to return it. The water will spill and the kappa will be defeated. As well, for some long-forgotten reason, kappas love cucumbers almost as they love human blood. A gift of a cucumber may win the friendship of a kappa, who might then reveal secrets about medicine.

See also:
Beasts
Grindylows
Merpeople

What Is the Most Important Language for Wizards?

Latin

U NLIKE MANY SCHOOLS, HOGWARTS DOES not seem to emphasize learning foreign languages – at least not in its first few years. But there is one language that even first-year students encounter often: Latin. Many charms, spells, and curses used throughout Rowling's *Harry Potter* books are close to or exactly the same as Latin words for the desired effect. For instance 'Lumos', the spell that causes a light to appear at the end of a wizard's wand, comes from the Latin word *lumen* meaning 'light'. 'Nox', the spell that extinguishes a wand's light, is Latin for 'night' or 'darkness'.

Latin is used in other places also. For example, Mad-Eye Moody was once an Auror, a sort of police officer whose job is to bring bad wizards to justice. In Latin, *aurora* means 'dawn', so Auror is the perfect name for someone who fights darkness. As well, the

Historians say the oldest example of Latin is four words engraved on a fancy cloak pin from the sixth or seventh century BC, which translate as: 'Manius made me for Numerius'.

Hogwarts motto is Latin: *Draco dormiens nunquam titillandus* ('Never tickle a sleeping dragon'). J. K. Rowling herself has said that she wanted her wizards to use a dead language as a living language. It makes sense that Latin would be so important. After the Romans conquered Europe and Britain about two thousand years ago, Latin became a common language, one that could be used anywhere in the empire. Scholars relied on it to ensure that their work could be shared. It was also the primary language of Christianity. And for centuries, most books were written in Latin, because every educated person could be expected to know it.

LATIN FOR WIZARDS

Here are a few spells from J. K. Rowling's *Harry Potter* books that come from Latin:

Accio: Summoning charm. From the Latin *accio*, meaning 'I call' or 'I summon'.

Aparecium: Makes invisible ink appear. From *appareo*, 'I make visible'.

Conjunctivitis Curse: Impairs eyesight. From *coniungare*, 'to bind together'. Eyes have connective tissue called the conjunctiva. When

Besides 'Avada Kedavra', the curses deemed 'Unforgivable' by the Ministry of Magic are: **'Crucio'**, which in Latin means 'I torture', and **'Imperio'**, which in Latin means 'I command'. (See **Avada Kedavra**).

this gets infected, a person gets conjunctivitis, commonly called 'pink eye'.

Deletrius: Makes things disappear. From *deleo*, 'I erase'.

Densaugeo: Makes teeth grow uncontrollably. From *dens*, meaning 'tooth', and *augeo*, 'I make grow.' (Draco Malfoy directs this curse to Harry, but it ricochets and instead hits Hermione.)

Diffindo: Splits things. From *diffindo*, 'I split [it] apart.'

Dissendium: Opens things, such as the statue of the witch that guards the secret passage from Hogwarts to Honeydukes. From *dissideo*, 'I separate.'

Enervate: Invigorates things. (Oddly, this spell's effect is the opposite of its meaning in both Latin and English. In English, 'enervate' means to weaken; and its Latin root, *enervo*, means the same. Neither means energize.)

Expecto Patronum: Produces a patronus (a guardian). From *especto*, 'I await' and *patronus*, 'a guardian'.

Responding to ***vox populi*** ('voice of the people', as in popular opinion), J. K. Rowling's publisher is offering Latin translations of Harry's adventures. The first, *Harrius Potter et Philosophi Lapis*, translated by Peter Needham, has been lauded* by Latin experts who say it is written in a style that is anything but dead.

[*'praised', from the Latin *laudare*.]

Expelliarmus: Disarms an opponent. From the Latin *expello*, 'I drive out' (or 'expel'); and *arma*, 'weapon'.

Fidelius Charm: Places a secret in another trusted person. From *fidelis*, 'faithful', 'trusted', 'trustworthy'.

Finite Incantatem: Ends others' spells. From *finite*, 'end'; and *incantantem*, 'incantation' or 'spell'.

Impedimenta: Stops a person or thing. From *impedimentum*, impediment, hindrance.

Incendio: 'I set aflame.' Used to travel by Floo from fireplace to fireplace. From *incendia*, 'fire'.

Obliviate: Makes a person forget. From *oblivio*, 'oblivion', 'forgetfulness'.

Petrificus Totalus: Immobilizes a person. From *petrificare*, 'to petrify' (derived from *petra*, 'rock'), and *totaliter*, 'entirely'.

Prior Incantatem: Reveals the previous spell cast by a wand. From *prior*, 'prior' or 'previous'; and *incantatem*, 'incantation' or 'spell'.

As a general rule of magic, successfully performing a spell requires more than just saying a few words. How the spell is spoken can have great consequence. Casting a spell can require an enormous amount of energy, so a wizard's power is an important factor.

Rictusempra: Tickles. From *rictus*, 'a laughing smile', and *semper*, 'always'.

Riddikulus: Makes something seem funny. Used to dispel a boggart. From *ridiculus*, 'laughable'.

Ruparo: Repairs things. From *reparo*, 'I repair'.

Wingardium Leviosa. Can make something fly. From *levis*: 'light' (which gives us the English word 'levitate').

LATIN FOR EVERYONE

Though most spells and curses are just single words, Latin can be used as an everyday language. In fact, it is still the official language of the Vatican. In an amusing book titled *Latin for All Occasions*, author Henry Beard offers a few expressions one might find useful:

What's happening?
Quid fit?

My dog ate it.
Canis meus id comedit.

It was that way when I got here.
Ita erat quando hic adveni.

Two wizarding skills Harry encounters in *Phoenix* have names with Latin roots. **Legilimency**, mind reading, comes from *legere*, 'to read', and *mens*, meaning 'mind' or 'thoughts'. **Occlumency**, preventing one's mind from being read with Legilimency, comes from *occludo*, 'I close down'.

Your fly is open.
Braccae tuae aperiuntur.

Rad, dude!
Radicitus, comes!

No way.
Nullo modo.

Fat chance.
Fors fortis.

Read my lips.
Labra lege.

Accidentally on purpose.
Casu consulto.

See also:
Malfoy Names

In addition, Beard offers this bumper sticker: SI HOC ADFIXUM IN OBICE LEGERE POTES, ET LIBERALITER EDUCATUS ET NIMIS PROPINQUUS ADES. It means: 'If you can read this bumper sticker, you are both very well educated and much too close.'

Why Is Each Malfoy Aptly Named?

J. K. ROWLING MUST HAVE HAD FUN CHOOSING names for the villainous Malfoys. Each one is loaded with meaning and history.

The family name derives from the Latin *maleficus*, meaning evil-doer. In medieval times the word was used to describe witches, whose evil acts were called maleficia. Witchcraft scholar Rosemary Ellen Guiley writes: 'In its narrowest definition, *maleficia* meant damage to crops and illness or death to animals. In its broadest, it included anything with a negative impact upon a person: loss of love, storms, insanity, disease, bad luck, financial problems, lice infestations, even death. If a villager muttered a threat or a wish for calamity upon someone and misfortune of any sort occurred to the victim – *maleficia*. If the local wise woman administered a remedy for an illness and the patient worsened or died – *maleficia*. If a hail storm destroyed the crop, the cows wouldn't give milk or the horse went lame – *maleficia*.' One of the first books on witchcraft and sorcery, the most significant of its time, was titled *Malleus Maleficarum* ('The Witch's Hammer'). Published in 1486, it was written by two witch hunters to help others catch witches. For two hundred years it was the most popular book after the Bible. The Latin word has been preserved in many languages. For instance, *maleficent* in English is defined as harmful or evil in intent or effect. *Mal foi* is French for 'bad faith'.

Draco has a double meaning in Latin, both 'dragon' and 'snake'. (Many languages used the same word for both.) Not surprisingly, Draco Malfoy is a Slytherin.

Draco's father is Lucius Malfoy – an echo of 'Lucifer', which has come to be a name for the Devil. That fits Lucius, a powerful Death Eater.

Draco's mother is Narcissa. Her name comes from Greek myth. The story goes that a handsome young man named Narcissus was very vain, so he was cursed by a god to fall in love with himself. Narcissus fell into a river while admiring his own reflection and drowned.

In 1484, the authors of *Malleus Maleficarum* were instructed by Pope Innocent VIII to prosecute witches in Germany.

See also:
Goyle
Names

Why Won't Wizards Go Near a Manticore?

In J. K. ROWLING'S *Harry Potter and the Prisoner of Azkaban*, Hermione, trying to find a legal ruling that will save Buckbeak the hippogriff, comes across a revealing reference: 'This might help, look – a manticore savaged someone in 1296, and they let the manticore off – oh – no, that was only because everyone was too scared to go near it.'

That's not surprising. The manticore may be the nastiest magical creature. A combination of man and beast, with sharp teeth and a vicious manner, it supposedly lived throughout ancient Asia. A frightening description was sketched in the second century by a Roman historian who drew from reports written as much as seven hundred years earlier:

'Manticore' comes from the Persian word *martikhora*, meaning **'man-eater'**.

There is in India a wild beast, powerful, daring, as big as the largest lion, of a red colour like cinnabar, shaggy like a dog,

149

and in the language of India it is called Martichoras. Its face however is not that of a wild beast but of a man, and it has three rows of teeth set in its upper jaw and three in the lower; these are exceedingly sharp and larger than the fangs of a hound. Its ears also resemble a man's, except that they are larger and shaggy; its eyes are blue-grey and they too are like a man's, but its feet and claws, you must know, are those of a lion.

To the end of its tail is attached the sting of a scorpion, and this might be over a cubit [eighteen inches] in length; and the tail has stings at intervals on either side. But the tip of the tail gives a fatal sting to anyone who encounters it, and death is immediate.

If one pursues the beast it lets fly its stings, like arrows, sideways, and it can

Manticore, from a 1607 woodcut.

shoot a great distance; and when it discharges its stings straight ahead it bends its tail back; if however it shoots in a backwards direction, then it stretches its tail to its full extent. Any creature that the missile hits it kills; the elephant alone it does not kill. These stings which it shoots are a foot long and the thickness of a bulrush. One writer asserts (and he says that the Indians confirm his words) that in the places where those stings have been let fly others spring up, so that this evil produces a crop.

According to the same writer the Manticore devours human beings; indeed it will slaughter a great number; and it lies in wait not for a single man but would set upon two or even three men, and alone overcomes even that number.

The Indians hunt the young of these animals while they are still without stings in their tails, which they then crush with a stone to prevent them from growing stings. The sound of their voice is as near as possible that of a trumpet.

A more recent description comes from the famous French poet and novelist of the nineteenth century, Gustave Flaubert. In *The*

Carol Rose, an expert in magical creatures, says in the Middle Ages the manticore was thought to be a representative of the prophet **Jeremiah**. This connection derived from the belief that the manticore lived deep in the Earth. Jeremiah had been imprisoned in a dungeon.

Temptation of Saint Anthony, Flaubert's manticore makes this colourful announcement: 'The gleam of my scarlet hair mingles with the reflection of the great sands. I breathe through my nostrils the terror of solitudes. I spit forth plague. I devour armies when they venture into the desert. My claws are twisted like screws, my teeth shaped like saws, and my curving tail bristles with darts, that I cast to right and left, before and behind. Look out!'

See also:
Beasts

Why Is the Third Task Set in a Maze?

Tᴴᴱ ᴛʜɪʀᴅ ᴀɴᴅ ꜰɪɴᴀʟ ᴛᴀꜱᴋ ᴏꜰ ᴛʜᴇ Triwizard Tournament is set within a maze built just for that purpose. Within it the competitors encounter a boggart, a sphinx, a Blast-Ended Skrewt, a giant spider, and a golden mist that turns them upside down. At the centre is the Triwizard Cup.

Tʜᴇ Lᴀʙʏʀɪɴᴛʜ ᴏꜰ Cʀᴇᴛᴇ

The maze – or labyrinth – is central to one of the best-known Greek myths about a hero's test of skill, the story of Theseus and the Minotaur. That labyrinth was built on the island of Crete by Daedalus, perhaps the most able inventor of his time. It was created to hold the pet of King Minos – a man-eating monster with a bull's head and a human body, known as the Minotaur.

At the time, Crete dominated Athens, which was forced to pay an annual tribute of

The **Minotaur**, from a vase of the fifth century BC.

seven young men and seven young women to Crete. Every year these unlucky souls were sent into the labyrinth, which was too confusing to escape, and were eaten by the Minotaur. One year, Theseus, son of the Athenian king, was among the offerings. But Minos's daughter Ariadne fell in love with him before he entered the labyrinth. To save his life, she gave him a sword to kill the Minotaur and a ball of thread to trail behind him so he could find his way back.

See also:
Centaurs
Fluffy

Although Theseus proved ungrateful to Ariadne, after his success in the labyrinth he became one of the greatest kings of Athens.

Why Might McGonagall Appear as a Cat?

THE VERY FIRST WIZARD TO APPEAR IN J. K. Rowling's *Harry Potter and the Philosopher's Stone* (even before Harry), is Minerva McGonagall, who lurks at Number Four Privet Drive in the form of a tabby cat. (A cat reading a map, actually – quite a shock to Mr Dursley, who isn't entirely sure if such a thing is possible or if, instead, it is 'a trick of the light'.)

Though Prof. McGonagall may become a cat because it best reflects her personality, a cat would be an appropriate choice for many witches and wizards. Cats are not only ancient civilized pets – domesticated for perhaps five thousand years – they have long been linked with magic. Being nocturnal, they naturally came to be associated with darkness, the moon, and the spirit world.

The Egyptian cat-goddess, **Bast**.

Cats were revered in the ancient cultures of Egypt and India, where mysticism originated. The city of Bubasti, at one time the capital of Egypt, was devoted to the worship of the cat-headed goddess, Bast. Hundreds of thousands of pilgrims flocked to the city each year. Cats were given elaborate funerals.

Sacred rituals also honoured cats in Europe. In ancient Rome, the goddess Diana had the power to transform herself into a cat. In Scandinavia, Freya, the Norse goddess of love, marriage, and fertility, was said to travel in a chariot drawn by two cats. Cats were also honoured in early British history. But as Christianity replaced paganism, cats became objects of scorn, fear and superstition.

When Mr Dursley stares at the tabby form of McGonagall, and she stares back, it's no surprise that Dursley senses (though only for a moment until his attention wanders!) an omen.

See also:

Animagus

Black, Sirius

Names

(McGonagall)

Why Might a Human Fear Merpeople?

FROM THE LATIN WORD *MARE*, MEANING 'sea', comes the name of these creatures known all over the world. The merpeople who live in the lake at Hogwarts, like so many others in literature, have green skin and long green hair. They have human torsos but silver fish tails instead of legs. (J. K. Rowling also adds some details that make her merpeople unique. Their houses are arranged in villages like those in the suburbs on land, and they make pets of grindylows.)

Legends of merpeople exist in nearly every culture. For instance, it was once said that the French aristocracy descended from a mermaid named Melusina.

As Rowling says in *Beasts*, the Sirens of Greek mythology are similar to mermaids.

157

They sing to the sailors of ships that pass by, enchanting them to their deaths on nearby rocks. In *The Odyssey*, Odysseus makes his crew plug their ears when they sail by the sirens, but orders them to tie him to the ship's mast so he can listen to the beautiful music without danger.

When Harry meets the merpeople during the second task of the Triwizard Tournament, he finds the same danger that contact with merpeople often symbolizes: the risk that the sea will prove so alluring that one will never return to land. As a character in one of the 'Twice-Told Tales' of the early American author Nathaniel Hawthorne tells a young woman, 'I fancied you akin to the race of mermaids, and thought how pleasant it would be to dwell with you among the quiet coves, in the shadows of the cliffs, and to roam along secluded beaches of the purest sand, and when our northern shores grew bleak, to haunt the islands, green and lonely, far amid summer seas.'

See also:
Beasts
Grindylows
Kappas

Why Are Mirrors Magical?

FOR THOUSANDS OF YEARS, THE FOLKLORE of wizards has mentioned mirrors. Being expensive to make in ancient times, mirrors were rare and had the power to inspire surprise and awe. According to some legends they were tools of the Devil, used for capturing souls just as they captured images. In the Middle Ages wizards stared into mirrors to see the future or answer great questions. This is called 'scrying'.

The most famous magical mirror in literature is the one belonging to the evil queen in *Snow White*. In a tale from *The Arabian Nights*, a genie gave Prince Alasnam a mirror that would reveal whether or not a lover could be trusted. In a poem from Elizabethan England, *The Faerie Queen*, Merlin created a mirror for King Ryence with similar powers:

John Dee (1527–1608), a favourite wizard of Britain's Queen Elizabeth I, often used a mirror for divination.

> *The great Magician Merlin had devised,*
> *By his deep science, and hell-dreaded might,*

Witchcraft
expert
Rosemary Ellen
Guiley found
a medieval
wizard's
instructions for
making a magic
mirror: 'Buy a
looking-glass
and inscribe
upon it
"S. Solam
S. Tattler
S. Echogordner
Gematur."
Bury it at a
crossroads
during an
uneven hour. On
the third day, go
to the spot at
the same hour
and dig it up –
but do not be
the first person
to gaze into it.
Let a dog or a
cat look first.'

A looking-glass, right wondrously built.
This mirror showed in perfect sight,
Whatever thing was in the world,
That the looker hoped to find;
Whatever foe had done, or friend or fiend,
Was thus discovered therein.

This mirror is very much like the one described by another famous British poet who lived three hundred years before Spenser. Geoffrey Chaucer – one of the first poets to write in English – created a long series of stories called *The Canterbury Tales*, each of which is narrated by a different fictional character making a pilgrimage to a shrine at Canterbury. In one of the stories, 'The Squire's Tale', a mirror is given to a king named Cambinskan from the King of Araby and Ind:

This mirror . . .
Has power such that men may in it see
Whether will come any adversity
Unto your realm, or yourself also;
And reveal who is your friend or foe.
And also this: if any lady bright
Has her heart set on any shining knight
If he is false, she shall his treason see.
And his other love, and all his secrecy.

MAGIC PORTALS

As well as tools for divination, mirrors are often portals to other worlds, like the one imagined by Lewis Carroll's Alice in *Through the Looking-glass*:

'Now, if you'll only wait, Kitty, and not talk so much, I'll tell you all my ideas about Looking-glass House. First, there's the room you can see through the glass – that's just the same as our drawing room, only the things go the other way . . . Let's pretend there's a way of getting through into it, somehow, Kitty. Let's pretend the glass has got all soft like gauze, so that we can get through. Why, it's turning into a sort of mist now, I declare! It'll be easy enough to get through –' She was up on the chimney-piece while she said this, though she hardly knew how she had got there. And certainly the glass was beginning to melt away, just like a bright mist.

There are many stories of people and monsters imprisoned in mirrors.

Most of all, mirrors are a reflection of the self, for better or worse. That is why they can be so dangerous. The Mirror of Erised in *Harry Potter and the Philosopher's Stone* is certainly this sort of mirror. J. K. Rowling says that it stands 'as high as the ceiling, with an ornate gold frame'. At the top the following words are carved: 'Erised stra ehru oyt ube cafru oyt on wohsi.' Obviously, this message is the mirror image of 'I show not your face but your heart's desire.' And what could be better than that? Anything, apparently, as Ron tells Harry: 'Dumbledore was right, that mirror could drive you mad.'

Although, as Rowling says, the Mirror of Erised is 'the key to finding the Stone', it is also a test of one's character. Vanity and self-ishness, central to the act of looking in a mirror, are corrupt qualities. Because only someone with rare virtue deserves his desire, only someone who looks in the mirror and sees others (as when Harry sees his parents in it) or sees himself committing a selfless act (such as keeping the Stone from Voldemort) will receive what he wishes.

Vulcan, the Roman god of fire and metalwork, was said to have a magic mirror that showed him scenes from the past, present, and future.

Which of Voldemort's Cohorts Comes from India?

IN *GOBLET*, VOLDEMORT IS KEPT ALIVE BY the poison of a large snake, Nagini. This is no ordinary snake. It has a royal bloodline and an important role in mythology.

Naga is Sanskrit for snake, and *nag* is the word for snake in several modern languages. In Buddhism and Hinduism, nagas are a race of semi-divine snakes with great powers. They live in a beautiful undergound city. Some have many heads. On the head of naga king Vasuki is a brilliant jewel, Nagamani, which has miraculous healing powers. In some legends the nagas are human from head to waist and serpent from the waist down. Female nagas are known as nagini.

A naga is said to have protected the Buddha, who was meditating under a tree during a great storm, by wrapping itself around him and spreading its heads to form an umbrella for him. As well, the world is said

A **naga**, from a Sri Lankan stone carving.

to rest on the many heads of a naga named Ananta. And the naga king, Vasuki, was used by the gods to churn the ocean to create Amrita, an elixir of immortality. Not coincidentally, this is just what Voldemort seeks.

Nagas share an interesting connection with the basilisk. Just as roosters are the enemy of a basilisk, the constant foe of the naga is Garuda, a powerful mythical bird.

See also:
Basilisk

Where Do Those Names Come From?!

DOES ANY WRITER CREATE NAMES WITH more care or a greater sense of humour than J. K. Rowling? She uses foreign words, puns, and anagrams; makes references to history and myth; takes names from maps and war memorials; and uses many flower names. Occasionally she makes up names out of thin air, but even that can be hard work. She says the name 'Quidditch' took almost two days of thinking and wordplay.

Rowling not only invents words, she invents fun histories for them. In *Quidditch Through the Ages*, written long after she introduced the game, she artfully answers the many queries of her fans by revealing that in Harry's world the game got its name from the place it was first played, Queerditch Marsh.

In at least one important case the origins are difficult for even Rowling to trace. She assumed she had invented 'Hogwarts'; but

J. K. Rowling says '**Harry**' is just a name she has always liked. It came to her instantly. '**Potter**' took longer. She tried several other names first. Her final choice came from the name of childhood friends.

after *Stone* was published, a friend of Rowling suggested to her that they had seen a plant named 'hog-wort' on a visit to the Royal Botanical Gardens at Kew. ('Wort' is an old word for 'plant', from the Anglo-Saxon *wyrt*.) That sounded right to Rowling. But Kew have no record of displaying the plant, an invasive weed of the sort they like to keep out, or the similarly-named 'hog-weed'. It's possible, say experts there, Rowling and her friend are recalling a pop song from their youth, 'The Return of the Giant Hogweed', by the band Genesis. It is a story about a very angry plant at the Gardens.

Rowling's own name is worth a little digging too. Just like the names inside the books, there's a story behind the name on the cover. 'J. K. Rowling' is partially invented. Rowling had no middle name before the first Harry Potter book was published. This became a problem when her publishers said they wanted the name on the book to have initials rather than 'Joanne'. (They worried boys would not want to read a book written by a woman.) 'J. Rowling' didn't sound right, so Rowling took the name of one of her grandmothers and then used its initial.

Here are some others, arranged by the sources Rowling commonly uses.

Rowling says **Ron Weasley** is a lot like her best friend from school; and his name is similar also. The boy who inspired Ron is named Sean.

Odd fact: He even had a Ford Anglia car.

Geography

Bagshot, Bathilda (the author of *A History of Magic*): Bagshot is a town near London.

Dursley: A town near J. K. Rowling's birth-place.

Firenze: Italian name for the city of Florence.

Flitwick, Professor (Charms teacher): Flitwick is a town in England.

Snape, Severus: Snape is the name of another English village.

Foreign Words

Bagman, Ludovic: In Latin, ludo means 'I play' – perfect for the head of the Department of Magical Games and Sports. 'Bagman' comes from his corrupt nature. In slang, a bagman is the person who handles the money in a dishonest scheme.

Beauxbatons: French for 'beautiful wands'.

Bonaccord, Pierre: The first Supreme Mugwump of the International Confederation of Wizards must have been a peacemaker, because in French his name means 'goodwill'

'Muggles' comes from English slang. A 'mug' can mean someone who is easily fooled. In 2003, J. K. Rowling's version was added to the Oxford English Dictionary.

or 'fellowship', or, literally, 'good agreement'. ('Mugwump' is the English version of *mugquomp*, meaning 'chief' in the language of the Algonquin tribe of Native Americans. It has also come to mean someone in politics who thinks independently.)

Gubraithian Fire: As Hermione explains to Harry and Ron in *Phoenix*, this is everlasting fire. The giants of the north probably knew this already, because Scots cheer *'Alba Gu Bragh!'* – 'Scotland Forever!' – in Gaelic. The name would also be recognized in Ireland, where people cheer *'Erin Go Bragh!'*

Mosag: Gaelic for nasty, dirty woman.

Nigellus, Phineas: His last name comes from the Latin word for 'black'. His first name refers to a Bible character, Phinehas, who was quick to accuse people of doing wrong. It's the perfect name for a character who storms about, complaining of everyone else's behaviour.

Tenebrus: The name of Hagrid's favourite Thestral comes from the Latin word meaning 'darkness' or 'blindness'. Many animals and insects that live in the dark have 'tenebrosus' in their scientific names.

Crookshanks: George Cruikshank (1792–1878) was a cartoonist who illustrated some of the most popular books of the nineteenth century, including the first English edition of Grimm's fairy tales and novels by Charles Dickens, Sir Walter Scott, and Louisa May Alcott. ('Cruikshank' and 'Crookshanks' literally mean 'bow-legged', as Crookshanks is.)

A George Cruikshank illustration.

Dearborn, Caradoc (Order of the Phoenix member who vanished and is thought to be dead): His last name is a translation of his first. 'Caradoc' means 'dearly loved'. In the legends of King Arthur a knight named

Caradoc is one of the most pure of the Round Table.

Diggory, Cedric: Digory Kirke is a hero of some of J. K. Rowling's favourite books as a child, *The Chronicles of Narnia* by C. S. Lewis. Notice that *Cedric* is not far from a rearrangement of *Kirke*.

Flint, Marcus (captain of the Slytherin Quidditch team): Possibly named for Captain John Flint from Robert Louis Stevenson's *Treasure Island*. (Rudolf Hein, creator of a web site devoted to Harry Potter names, made this clever connection.)

On many telephone keypads, the Ministry of Magic's **phone number**, 62442, spells M-A-G-I-C.

Granger, Hermione (pronounced her-MY-oh-nee): Her uncommon first name is a form of 'Hermes', name of the Greek god of communication and eloquence. It fits the talkative Ms Granger well. Rowling found the name in Shakespeare's *A Winter's Tale*, and makes a fun reference to Shakespeare's character in *Harry Potter and the Chamber of Secrets*. Shakespeare's Hermione is turned into a statue, which is what happens to Hermione Granger after the basilisk attacks her in *Chamber*. Rowling must have smiled when she thought of that. (See also 'Hermes', page 176)

Lockhart, Gilderoy: The first name of this phoney refers to his being gilded (covered in a thin gold foil) to make him seem intelligent and attractive. Rowling found it in a book that mentioned a legendary Gilderoy who was a handsome highway thief and something of a folk hero. The last name, she says, comes from a war memorial. Gilderoy Lockhart's hypnotic power over female fans happens to fit that last name, which means 'strong beguiler' and was shared by a Scottish nobleman whose proud motto was 'Locked hearts I open'.

(Although an Australian town called Lockhart is near another called Wagga Wagga, which gave its name to the Wagga Wagga Werewolf that Gilderoy fought, J. K. Rowling recalls that 'Lockhart' came first, and not from a map. Perhaps it's a coincidence; or perhaps she decided to connect the two when she saw 'Lockhart' on the map next to a name too good to resist.)

Marchbanks, Griselda (Wizengamot elder who resigns when Dolores Umbridge is appointed High Inquisitor of Hogwarts in *Phoenix*): Her last name comes from a pseudonym, 'Samuel Marchbanks', used by the Canadian novelist Robertson Davies. Like Rowling, Davies is known for stories that combine magic and

Rowling's source for the name 'Gilderoy' mentions a J. G. Lockhart who wrote many books, just like Rowling's Gilderoy. He was the son-in-law and biographer of Sir Walter Scott, the author whose skills earned him the nickname 'Wizard of the North'.

academic life. One of his books, *Tempest-Tost*, tells of a company of amateur actors putting on Shakespeare's play *The Tempest*, about a wizard and his enchanted island. The character in the novel who plays Shakespeare's heroine, Ariel, is named Griselda Webster.

McGonagall, Minerva: Her first name, as mentioned earlier, refers to Minerva, Roman goddess of wisdom and the arts. Her last name, Rowling admits, comes from William McGonagall (c. 1830–1902), a Scottish poet who is famous for being awful. Though people eventually grew fond of his determination, they also laughed at him a lot. But that didn't stop him. He was oblivious to his reputation.

Tofty, Professor: This wrinkled wizard, who helps Griselda Marchbanks conduct the OWL examinations in *Phoenix*, is no toff. Although it's possible Rowling just ran across the name somewhere, it's also possible there's a more amusing explanation connected to the source of Marchbanks's name described above. While the Robertson Davies novel *Tempest-Tost*, which offered Marchbank's name, is about Shakespeare's *The Tempest*, the phrase 'tempest-tost' actually appears in a line spoken by a witch in *Macbeth*. When plotting trouble for

from
'Loch Ness'
by William
McGonagall

Beautiful Loch
  Ness,
The truth to
  express,
Your landscapes
  are lovely and
  gay,
Along each side
  of your waters,
To Fort
  Augustus all
  the way,
Your scenery is
  romantic,
With rocks and
  hills gigantic,
Enough to make
  one frantic . . .

a character, she speaks the lines Davies quotes at the beginning of his book:

> *Though his bark* [boat] *cannot be lost,*
> *Yet it shall be tempest-tost* [tossed by a storm]
> (Act I, scene iii)

However, until modern times the letter 's' was sometimes written differently, as this detail from the first printed edition of *Macbeth* shows:

> **Though his Barke cannot be loſt,**
> **Yet it ſhall be Tempeſt-toſt.**

Weird Sisters: The name of Harry's favourite musical group is another Shakespeare reference. It appears several times in *Macbeth* to describe the three witches who help stir up trouble in their cauldron.

HISTORY

Doge, Elphias (founding member of the Order of the Phoenix): His first name is a small twist on Eliphas Levi, the pseudonym of French sorcerer and author Alphonse Louis Constant (1810–1875), whose many books on magic were popular and influential. 'Doge'

The witches in *Macbeth* were not Shakespeare's invention. They appear in his source, Raphael Holinshed's 'Chronicles of England, Scotland, and Ireland' (1577). Even the phrase **'weird sisters'** appears in Holinshed. He explained the women as 'the goddesses of destiny [the Fates], or else some nymphs or fairies with knowledge of prophecy' though magic.

was the name of the leader or 'duke' of Venice when it was a republic. In *Phoenix*, Sirius shows Harry a photo of Elphias and points out 'that stupid hat', a reference to the famous symbol of the doge, a cap called a *corno* ('horn' in Italian).

Slytherin, Salazar: António de Oliveira Salazar was dictator of Portugal – where J. K. Rowling once lived – from 1932 to 1968. He was known for very harsh policies. (Another smart connection made by Rudolf Hein.)

Costume of the **Doge** of Venice, with corno.

Smethwyck, Hippocrates: The Healer-in-Charge in one of St Mungo's wards gets his first name from an ancient Greek physician who is considered the founder of medical science. The oath that doctors take today is called the Hippocratic Oath.

Violet: This gossipy witch, who zips from painting to painting in *Goblet*, eavesdropping on the conversation with the four Triwizard Tournament champions and then racing to tell the Fat Lady what she has heard, is not named for a flower. (The violet flower signifies modesty, which hardly fits her.) The clue to her identity may be the 'walrus moustache' on the man in the painting next to hers. A woman named Violet Hunt (1866–1942) was a notorious literary figure in early twentieth century England, known as much for her flirtatiousness and unreliable gossip as for her writing. She had a long, complicated, and very public love affair with novelist Ford Madox Ford, who had a very full walrus moustache of his own.

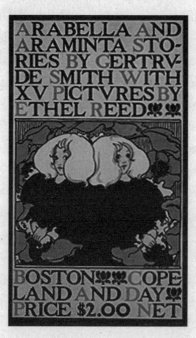

J. K. Rowling is not the only writer to choose odd names like **Araminta** (for a relative of Sirius) and **Arabella** (the first name of Mrs Figg). Maybe she just thinks they sound good – that's to say, they're 'mellifluous', like Araminta **Meliflua**. In the 1895 novel pictured to the left, well known for its illustrations, Arabella and Araminta are twin sisters.

Wizengamot: This assembly of wizards takes its name from the Anglo-Saxon version of the House of Lords, the *Witenagemot*. In Anglo-Saxon that name literally means assembly (*gemot*) of wise men or counsellors (*witan*).

Diggle, Dedalus: In Greek myth, Daedalus was a brilliant inventor. Among his many designs was the Labyrinth of Crete that inspired the maze of the Triwizard Tournament (see page 153). When the king of Crete would not let Daedalus leave the island, he fashioned wings from feathers and wax for himself and his son Icarus. As they flew away Icarus became overconfident and flew too close to the sun, melting the wax and destroying the wings. He fell, and died. Daedalus, older and wiser, survived.

Hermes (Percy Weasley's owl): Hermes was the messenger of the Greek gods.

Jones, Hestia: When Harry first meets Order of the Phoenix member Hestia Jones she is near a toaster. That's a joke about her first name. In Greek mythology, Hestia is the goddess of the hearth (the fireplace where meals are cooked).

Lupin, Remus (a werewolf): The name of this werewolf is a double pun. *Lupus* is Latin for 'wolf'. The legendary founders of Rome, who as children were suckled by a wolf, were named Romulus and Remus.

Meadowes, Dorcas (late member of the Order of the Phoenix): Dorcas is a Bible character, also known as Tabitha, noted for her good deeds. Many churches have a Dorcas Society made of female members who help the poor.

Patil, Parvati: Parvati is a Hindu goddess.

Prewett, Gideon: This founding member of the Order of the Phoenix gets his first name from a Bible character who fought the followers of what was thought to be a false god, Baal.

Ragnok: If his name is any indication, the goblin with whom Bill Weasley is negotiating an alliance against Voldemort in *Phoenix* would be a fierce friend. It comes from Ragnorok, Norse mythology's version of the Apocalypse, a great battle that ends the world as we know it.

Sprout, Pomona: The first name of the Hogwarts professor of Herbology comes from the Roman goddess of fruit. Her last name needs no explanation. (Close readers will notice the name 'Pomona' has not yet appeared in the novels. However, it is on one of the official wizard cards made from J. K. Rowling's character histories.)

Ragnorok ends when Fenrir, a terrifying wolf-monster who is the child of the trickster god Loki, swallows the sun, symbol of the chief Norse god, Odin. This myth was the basis of key scenes in J. R. R. Tolkien's *The Lord of the Rings* and *The Silmarillion*.

Tonks, Nymphadora: 'The first name of this shape-shifting wizard refers to nymphs, nature spirits in Greek mythology whose name was later connected to creatures that change their form as they grow. (See page 30)

SAINTS

Hedwig: A saint who lived in Germany in the twelfth and thirteenth centuries. An order of nuns established under her patronage chose as its work the education of orphaned children – like Harry.

Ronan (centaur): An Irish saint. (As some readers have pointed out, Ronan the centaur has red hair!)

St Mungo's Hospital for Magical Maladies and Injuries: A real St Mungo's in London is a large humanitarian organization for the homeless. Saint Mungo is the patron saint of Glasgow, Scotland, and appears on its coat of arms.

FLOWERS AND PLANTS

Brown, Lavender (one of Hermione's roommates): In legend the lavender flower has many meanings. One of them, which fits Lavender Brown's childish way of gossiping with her friend Parvati Patil, is distrust.

Delacour, Fleur: In French, *fleur* is simply 'flower'. With '*de la cour*' it means 'flower of the court', a term for a noblewoman.

Dursley, Petunia: The petunia symbolizes anger and resentment. Enough said.

Figg, Arabella: The fig flower signifies secrets. Arabella is certainly keeping one.

Malfoy, Narcissa: The narcissus flower, which shares its name with the vain Narcissus of Greek legend, symbolizes self-love, a typical Malfoy quality. (See page 148)

Moaning Myrtle: The Myrtle symbolizes joy, a funny twist for the name of this unhappy ghost.

Oliver Wood (the Quidditch player), Olive Hornby (the student who teased Moaning Myrtle), and Mr Ollivander (wand maker): Oliver Wood deserves the connection between olive laurels and victory. Olive Hornby certainly isn't connected to the other meaning of the olive tree, peace, but perhaps some of Mr Ollivander's wands are.

Parkinson, Pansy: The pansy signifies thinking

of a loved one. While it's true that Pansy Parkinson thinks of Draco Malfoy after the incident with Buckbeak in *Azkaban*, most of the time she doesn't think of anyone but herself. Instead, look to the word's modern slang meaning, an annoying girlishness.

Patil, Padma: *Padma* is the Sanskrit word for the lotus flower, central to Hindu religion. It is a common name.

Pomfrey, Poppy: The first name of the Hogwarts nurse comes from the flower of the opium plant, which has long been used as medicine. (See also page 66)

Potter, Lily: The lily is a symbol of purity, which makes it almost too perfect for the name of Harry's mother.

Spore, Phyllida (author of *One Thousand Magical Herbs*): From the 'spores' plants use as seeds, and the Greek *phylla*, meaning 'leaves'.

MISCELLANEOUS

N.E.W.T.s (Nastily Exhausting Wizarding Tests): Newts, baby salamanders, are familiar to witches and wizards from the brew mixed in

Plants and trees also appear in the names of the streets in the Dursley's town of Little Whinging: The Durselys live on **Privet** Drive. Mrs Figg lives on **Wisteria** Walk. The Knight Bus stops at **Magnolia** Crescent. Dudley and his friends gang up on Harry in **Magnolia** Road.

Shakespeare's *Macbeth*: 'Eye of newt and toe of frog, wool of bat and tongue of dog.' (See also pages 126 and 127)

Diagon Alley: Typical of everything in the wizard world, this street doesn't run straight; it runs 'diagonally'.

Dumbledore, Aberforth: The first name of Albus Dumbledore's missing brother is an old word meaning 'to wander off', or, even more worrisome given the lure of Voldemort's power, to 'stray off the path'.

Filibuster, Dr: The fireworks maker gets his name from a trick politicians use to stop a debate. They talk for hours or even days without letting anyone interrupt. Unlike fireworks, filibusters usually end not with a bang but a whimper.

Grey, Lady: Ravenclaw's house ghost is named for a specific type of spirit. Many mansions and castles are said to be haunted by a 'Grey Lady' from a local family, who, when alive, had been unlucky in love or lost a partner.

Grimmauld Place (the Black family resi-

'Oswald', the middle name of **Cornelius Fudge**, refers not to American assassin Lee Harvey Oswald but to Oswald Mosely, once the leader of Britain's fascists. Mosely and his wife were close friends with Adolf Hitler and shared his views.
(Ironically, Diana Mosely's sister, who held the opposite views, was author Jessica Mitford, Rowling's self-described 'heroine'.)

dence): It's grim. It's old. It's a grim old place. Yes, some books of magical history say Oliver Cromwell (1599–1658), Lord Protector of England, may have a supernatural ally named 'Grimoald'. But don't bet on that having any meaning.

Hagrid, Rubeus: 'Hagrid' is an old term for someone who looks worse for wear – as if they had been ridden by a hag. 'Rubeus' is Latin for 'red', because of Hagrid's ruddy face. His habit of indulging in one too many drinks would account for both names.

Carl Jung said people who believe in magicians and wizards were just making **imagoes** of powerful people they didn't understand.

Hopkirk, Mafalda (head of the Improper Use of Magic Office): In Portugal, where J. K. Rowling once lived, 'Mafalda' is the name of a hugely popular comic strip character. (The name fits the cartoon character, a headstrong young girl: 'Mafalda', the Portuguese form of 'Matilda', means 'mighty in battle'.) 'Hopkirk' may well be a humorous reference to 'Randall and Hopkirk (Deceased)' a comedy-detective show that aired on television when J. K. Rowling was a child and still has a cult following. It certainly had a connection to magic. One of the detectives, Hopkirk, was a ghost.

Imago, Inigo (author of *The Dream Oracle*):

The term 'imago' was adopted by psychologist Carl Jung (pronounced 'yoong') to describe a false, ideal image of someone important – usually a parent. Like Inigo Imago, Jung is known for theories about interpreting dreams. 'Inigo' sounds like it would be related to 'imago', but it is simply an old name. It is common in Spain, and one of Britain's greatest architects was Inigo Jones (1573–1652).

Jigger, Arsenius (author of *Magical Drafts and Potions*): Arsenic is a poison used in many magical concoctions. A jigger is a liquid measurement, a bit more than a fluid ounce.

Knockturn Alley: This unsavoury street, where shops like Borgin & Burkes cater to those who pursue the Dark Arts, is a place you wouldn't want to visit 'nocturnally'.

Metamorphmagus: a simple combination of 'metamorphosis', meaning transformation, and 'magus', meaning wizard. (See page 30)

Skeeter, Rita: Fitting for an annoying (and blood-sucking) bug one wants to swat!

Squib: Wizard-born humans who lack magical powers are called by this term for fireworks

Rowling has answered a question that puzzled many readers of *Phoenix*. if Harry saw his parents die, why hadn't he seen the **thestrals** before? She explained that the death has to 'sink in' before the creatures become visible.

that fizzle and disappoint.

Thestrals: These (usually) invisible animals get their name from an Anglo-Saxon word, *thester*, meaning 'darkness' or 'make dark'.

See also:
Dumbledore
Hogwarts

Widdershins, Willy: The prankster who plays tricks with Muggle toilets in *Phoenix* gets his unusual last name from a magic ritual. 'Widdershins' is an old word meaning anti-clockwise, and witches often 'walk widder-shins' – in an anti-clockwise circle – while doing magic.

What Were the Models for the Order of the Phoenix?

WHEN THE TITLE OF HARRY'S FIFTH adventure was announced, two years before the book appeared, everyone who enjoys hunting for J. K. Rowling's clues saw a big one: the phrase 'Order of the Phoenix' brings to mind many classical references. But when the book finally appeared, the title proved less revealing than expected. The Order she created does have classical sources, but it is also rich in wordplay from the present day that conceals a modern meaning.

There is a real Order of the Phoenix. It is an honour given by the Greek government to foreign citizens who have aided Greece in some way.

'WE STAND ON GUARD FOR THEE'
In literature as in history, any group calling itself an 'order' can be expected to have a purpose. The Order of the Knights of the Temple ('Knights Templar') was founded in 1119 to guard pilgrims travelling to the Holy Land. Knights and Ladies in modern Britain are officially members of the Order of the Garter,

185

The members of one legendary order don't even know it exists. In Jewish lore there are 36 honest men, scattered around the world, known as the **Lamed Wufniks**. These men carry in themselves the best virtues of humankind, and their example reminds God that mankind is not completely evil. But if one ever learns of his role he must die and another must take his place.

founded in 1348 to set a standard for chivalry and bring knights under greater influence of the monarchy. The Order of the Star, founded in 1352, was intended to do the same in France.

In stories of fantasy and adventure, an order nearly always acts as a secret guardian of a cause. Fantasy literature experts John Clute and John Grant outline the pattern: members defend their world or sometimes the entire world; they actively battle evil rather than just

waiting for it pass; and they risk their lives for their beliefs. As Clute and Grant add, 'Secret Guardians are the standard opponents of dark lords and potential dark lords'.

WISDOM OF OUR ELDERS
The Order of the Phoenix also falls into a special category of secret guardians that Clute and Grant call 'Pariah Elite'. These orders survive on the fringe of their societies, 'despised and

rejected' because the rest of the world is already falling under the influence of the enemy. Dumbledore and his friends are ridiculed and harassed by most other wizards, including the powerful politicians Cornelius Fudge and Dolores Umbridge.

However, like other Pariah Elites, the Order survives because it has special knowledge. It understands its enemies better than they understand themselves. And in remaining true to the old ways it benefits from ancient secrets that other wizards have forgotten – for example, how to move around without using the Floo Network, which is being watched by Fudge's spies.

LULLABY OF BIRDLAND

Anyone who tried to guess what might come in *Phoenix* would have been right to rely on certain universal ideas. What about the 'Phoenix' in the name? Would it be a reference to Dumbledore's pet, Fawkes? Would it have anything to do with ancient Egypt, where the legend of the phoenix began? Scholars have filled whole books with the symbolism of the bird, so there are plenty of clues to be found there. The phoenix is a symbol of immortality, which is Voldemort's great desire, so perhaps

The Knights Templar gained great power and influence, leading Europe's kings to fear them. And being in the Holy Land, they developed relations with Muslims, which made Christians suspicious. Eventually resentment grew so strong their power was said to come from witchcraft practised in secret rituals. In the early 1300s the king of France joined with the Pope to destroy them.

that would be the secret the Order guards? Or would it suggest that the Order of the Phoenix is linked to the very beginnings of magical knowledge in Egypt? In real life, even recently, there have been secret societies based on Egyptian magic. The Rosicrucians, formed in the 1600s, have been the subject of many novels. The Hermetic Order of the Golden Dawn, established in 1888, claimed to draw its knowledge from an ancient manuscript the founder discovered and deciphered. (One branch was headed by the poet W. B. Yeats, who was fascinated by the spirit world.)

If Dumbledore had any of these ideas in mind when he formed the order to organize resistance to Voldemort, he hasn't shared them with Harry yet. But J. K. Rowling has shared some of her ideas about the group in the form of clues hidden in the member's names.

A Twist in the Tale

You may have noticed a mix of old and new characters in the Order. New ones include Emmeline Vance and Kingsley Shacklebolt. The Prewetts have been mentioned before, but in *Phoenix* they are referred to for the first time by their given names, Gideon and Fabian. Other characters mentioned briefly in the past are now revealed to have important roles in

Kingsley **Shacklebolt's** last name comes from an old word for handcuffs. Shacklebolts appear on many family crests as a symbol of victory in battle.

the plot. These characters point to a real-life 'order' that J. K. Rowling had in mind, at least for her own amusement, when she created the Order of the Phoenix.

Surprisingly, the group had nothing to do with magic. It is a famous group of intellectuals that included as members or close associates some of the leading authors of the time: George Bernard Shaw; H. G. Wells; Beatrix Potter; and Edith Nesbit, who J. K. Rowling says was one of her favourite authors as a child.

One of its founders was a man named Frank Podmore, who happened to have straw-coloured hair just like Sturgis Podmore. A later member was Kingsley Martin, editor of a political journal called *The New Statesman*. One of its more notorious members was Emmeline Pankhurst, Britain's most energetic fighter on behalf of women's rights. (She was arrested twelve times in one year alone.) Emmeline Vance is wearing a green shawl when Harry first sees her, bringing to mind the standard millworker's shawl and clogs that suffragettes wore during protests and the colours the movement adopted as symbols: white to signify purity, purple to mean dignity, and green for hope.

And what is the name of this group? The

'Vance' means 'forward', so it fits a progressive activist. (Coincidentally, the German word *Wanze*, pronounced like 'vance', describes people who are irritating, as many activists mean to be. It literally means 'bedbug'!)

clue is in the name of wizard Fabian Prewett. It is the Fabian Society.

PATIENCE IS A VIRTUE

Separate from their political activities, Fabian Society founders Frank Podmore and Edward Pease were interested in things such as ghosts and telepathy. They met when both went to see for themselves if a ghost would appear as promised at a house in London. As they suspected, it didn't.

The Fabian Society was founded in 1884 to promote social justice. At the time, most socialists were heavily influenced by the ideas of Karl Marx and others who believed that only a revolution, and probably a bloody one, could lead to fair government and a decent life for the poor. The Fabians believed differently. They took their name from a Roman general, Fabius Maximus, known as 'Cunctator', which is Latin for 'the Delayer'. In one of Rome's wars Fabius had resisted urgent advice to attack the Carthaginian general Hannibal, believing it was smarter to move slowly and let time work against his foe. He turned out to be right. In the same way, the founding Fabians believed that time is on the side of those fighting for social justice. They would influence the system rather than attack it. A motto that appeared to be taken from a Roman history but was probably penned by Podmore said: 'For the right moment you must wait, as Fabius did most patiently, when warring against Hannibal, though many censured his delays; but when the time comes you must strike hard, as Fabius did, or your waiting will be in vain and fruitless.' That sounds like someone with both the patience and the determination we expect from Dumbledore.

The society still exists and plays an important role in British politics. In 1900, the Fabian Society and trade unions formed the Labour Party. Fabians in Parliament have included prime ministers Ramsay MacDonald, Clement Attlee, Harold Wilson and Tony Blair. Political scientist Harold Laski was a Fabian. (A full list of recognizable names could run pages.)

MONUMENTAL PROBLEMS

But does it really make sense that Rowling would think of this sort of reference, even for fun? What do politics have to do with the story? Only everything, as J. K. Rowling's comments reveal.

The battle between Dumbledore's Order of the Phoenix and Cornelius Fudge's Ministry of Magic is a battle between people who truly believe in fairness and those who just use it as a word to satisfy the public. The Ministry would claim that the huge statue of the wizard and magical beasts at its headquarters celebrates the fair society the Ministry has created. Dumbledore says it is a lie – and one that will come back to haunt the wizards. A divided society cannot fight Voldemort, just as the stu-

The Fabian Society was *not* headquartered on a 'Grimmauld Place'. Its base was Podmore's house at 14 Dean's Yard, Westminster.

dents were warned by the Sorting Hat's song in *Phoenix*. Harry has already suffered some disastrous consequences. As Dumbledore explains to Harry, the great loss at the end of *Phoenix* came about because of the warped treatment of Kreacher, the Black family's house elf.

Is it hard to believe someone who writes children's books would care so much about politics? Edith Nesbit did. Beatrix Potter did. So did the adult book author that J. K. Rowling has identified many times as her 'heroine', Jessica Mitford.

And as for J. K. Rowling, consider this: when she was asked where she'd like to visit if she had an invisibility cloak like Harry's, she replied, '10 Downing Street would be a good start.'

See also

Death Eaters

Besides Mail, What Does the Arrival of an Owl Mean?

OWLS, OF COURSE, ARE THE PRIMARY means of communication between wizards in Harry's world. But in our world, even though everyone likes to get mail, not everyone welcomes owls. Many cultures, such as Egyptian, Roman and Aztec, were ambivalent about this bird of prey. In several parts of the world an owl's screech is considered a bad omen, perhaps even of death. As well, owls, being nocturnal, have long been associated

J. K. Rowling says she found the name for **Hedwig**, Harry's owl, in a book of saints (see **Names**).

with sorcery, which is always certain to scare someone.

Nonetheless, some cultures embraced this bird. The emblem of Athens was an owl, because so many lived there. There was an ancient saying, 'Don't send owls to Athens', referring to a silly waste of effort. Today one might hear a similar phrase, 'Don't carry coal to Newcastle', because Newcastle was traditionally a coal-mining town.

Because Athens was a centre of learning, owls also came to symbolize intelligence. They were even adopted as the emblem of Minerva, Roman goddess of wisdom (counterpart to the Greek goddess Athena, patron of Athens).

Ron's small owl, **Pigwidgeon**, gets its name from a tiny fairy.

Could Snape's Potions Actually Work?

FOUR HUNDRED YEARS AGO WILLIAM Shakespeare offered a recipe as awful as anything simmering on Snape's stove. His play *Macbeth* included characters that are schemers, liars, and even murderers, but to make the story even more grim he introduced a chorus of three witches brewing something to 'double, double' the plot's 'toil and trouble':

> *First Witch:* Round about the cauldron go;
> In the poison'd entrails [intestines]
>   throw.
> Toad, that under cold stone
> Days and nights hast thirty-one
> Swelter'd [sweaty] venom
>   sleeping got,
> Boil thou first i' the charmed pot.
>   *All:* Double, double toil and trouble;
> Fire burn and cauldron bubble.

Shakespeare's disgusting list is also a catalogue of puns. His audiences knew some of the animal parts referred to plants that had odd names. Toe of frog meant the buttercup; wool of bat was moss; tongue of dog was hound's tongue; scale of dragon was bistort leaves; witches' mummy was mandrake; baboon's blood was a type of sap. (See **Herbology**)

As they chant and stir the pot they add more magical scraps: a newt's eye; a frog's toe; a lizard's leg; bat hair; the forked tongue of a snake; the wing of a small owl; the scale of a dragon; the tooth of a wolf; the mummy of a witch; a shark's jaw; a bit of poison hemlock; the liver, nose, lips and finger of some people they don't like; and the blood of a baboon. When it cools, one witch commands:

And now about the cauldron sing,
Like elves and fairies in a ring,
Enchanting all that you put in.

These witches would have no trouble with N.E.W.T. exams. This recipe is far more difficult than anything Harry faces in Snape's class. And why not? Through the ages, in real life as in literature, mixing a witch's brew has been a difficult art. The Greek sorceress Medea amazed the gods when she cooked up a batch of youth restorer using ingredients and charms no one could match.

JUST WHAT THE DOCTOR ORDERED
Although she has fun inventing and exaggerating just as Shakespeare did, the recipes for J. K. Rowling's potions, like everything else in her world, include a lot of history and legend.

Many items in Snape's cupboard are real. If you'd been alive just a few hundred years ago, the local doctor might have offered you a concoction made from ingredients Harry uses. Here are some tasty treats described in *The English Physician* by Nicholas Culpeper, a 1653 medical text that is still in print today after more than a hundred editions (DO NOT try them at home):

• For earaches, crushed millipedes and lice were mixed with wine and poured into the ear.

• For pain, the author recommended eating snakes. Burnt scorpions, he said, would cure kidney stones.

• Earthworm powder would make a tooth fall out quickly, as would the ashes of burnt ants and ant eggs.

• Eating grasshoppers supposedly cured a stomach-ache.

• Sea foam collected from the shore would cure baldness if you rubbed it on your head or make your teeth white if you brushed with it.

• To lose the desire for wine or beer you only had to drink a glass of it from a jug in which an eel had been placed to die. That probably also cured the desire for eels.

This may seem like harsh medicine compared to Madam Pomfrey's mixture of a little magic and a lot of chocolate. However, Harry

Culpeper's book was once required reading for any educated doctor. An equally popular book by Culpeper, *The Complete Herbal*, is the source and inspiration for the names of some of Rowling's plants. (See **Herbology**.)

has already learned about some very strong ingredients that doctors like Culpeper prescribed regularly.

Aconite. Also known as monkshood and wolfsbane, this is the key ingredient in Wolfsbane Potion, which prevents Remus Lupin from becoming a werewolf. Doctors once prescribed small doses of this herb to calm patients' nerves. It can be very poisonous in large doses, so hunters dipped spears and arrows in it to kill large animals. That's how it got the name wolfsbane. ('Bane' comes from the Old English *bana,* meaning destroyer or killer.) And because it worked against real wolves, a legend arose that it worked against werewolves, too.

Belladonna. Essence of Belladonna is mentioned in *Goblet.* The name, Italian for 'beautiful woman', refers to the women who used it to make their pupils larger and their skin paler, which they believed made them prettier. Also known as deadly nightshade, it can be quite poisonous. It has been used throughout history to calm the nerves and make patients go to sleep. In large doses it can make people experience strange visions, so it has long been associated with witches.

Bezoar. As Harry learns during his very first

Aconite was said to have been created by Hecate (pronounced 'HEK-u-tuh'), the Greek goddess of witchcraft, from the foamy saliva of Cerberus, the nasty three-headed dog that guarded the underworld.

Potions class in *Stone*, a bezoar is a 'stone' found in a goat's stomach, which works as poison antidote. Hard as it may be to believe, bezoars truly exist and were used just that way. They are hard balls of hair or undigested vegetable fibre sometimes found in the stomachs of animals like goats and cows, which chew cud. The name itself comes from Persian words meaning 'protector from poison'. In *The English Physician* it is described as such, as well as 'a notable restorer of nature . . . [that] makes a merry, blithe, cheerful creature.' There were many ways to prepare it. One cure for fever mixed bezoar with powdered deer's horn, crushed pearls, snakeskin, and crab's eyes and claws – all rolled into a ball with jelly. Perhaps that truly did make patients merry and cheerful; or perhaps they stopped complaining to avoid the dose.

Aconite, **belladonna**, and **hellebore** were said to be used in the mixture that was spread on **broomsticks** to make them fly.

Hellebore. In *Phoenix*, syrup of hellebore is used in the Draught of Peace. For thousands of years doctors have used hellebore the same way. A sedative, it was commonly given to people suffering a mental illness. It has been used this way for so long it even appears in a Greek myth. When the goddess Hera became angry with King Proetus of Tiryns, she made his daughters go mad. Under her spell they believed they were cows and wandered through pastures until a doctor cured them with hellebore.

Nettles. In *Stone*, Snape teaches the students to make a potion with nettles that will cure boils. This is just how doctors used the plant: to dry out sores. In *The English Physician* it is described in words Snape might use: 'singularly good to wash either old, rotten, or stinking sores and gangrenes [dying flesh], and such as fretting, eating, or corroding scabs, manginess, and itch, in any part of the body'.

Nettle tea was also recommended by doctors in the spring to cure the common cold. That may be what the witch Gertie Kettle had in mind when she picked nettles for tea in Queerditch Marsh, and thus became one of the first eyewitnesses to the game of Quidditch, as recounted in *Quidditch Through the Ages*.

Wormwood. This is an ingredient in the Draught of Living Death – for good reason. Wormwood gets its name because it was used to make a medicine that would kill stomach worms. However, it is more famous for the drink also made from it: absinthe, a green liquor that became notorious for causing so much harm to drinkers that it was outlawed in many countries. In the late 1800s many artists such as the painter Vincent Van Gogh and the writer Charles Beaudelaire claimed it gave them creative visions. Doctors believed it made drinkers go permanently mad.

PLEASE DON'T EAT THE DAISIES

Amazingly, some of the ingredients mentioned above are still used in medicines. In fact the pills and ointments we use today are often made from chemicals found in plants. And in many countries, herbalists still mix the natural ingredients.

Just as surprising as the real potion ingredients are the ones entirely from legend:

Asphodel. This is an ingredient in the 'Draught of Living Death' mentioned in *Stone.* In Greek mythology, the asphodel, a type of lily, was well known as the flower of the underworld and the dead. Persephone, queen of the underworld, loved the asphodel, and it was said that in the afterlife souls might walk in fields of it. Long ago it was eaten; and it was thought to be a favourite food of the dead, so it was planted near tombs.

Bicorn horn. Powder from it is an ingredient in Polyjuice Potion, the concoction that allows Ron and Harry to change into their

Most people dislike the taste of absinthe, which must be sweetened because **wormwood** is very bitter. It tastes so bad that a legend arose: when the evil serpent of the Bible was driven out of Paradise, wormwood began to grow where the snake had slithered.

Slytherin enemies Crabbe and Goyle in *Chamber*. The Bicorn is a mythical animal, said to eat only husbands who are pushed around by their wives. According to legend, it is very fat. (The legend is supposed to be funny. Don't blame me if it isn't.)

Daisy Roots. In *Azkaban*, the class makes Shrinking Solution using daisy roots. In legend it has long been thought that daisy-root potion makes a person small. The poem 'Kensington Garden', by Thomas Tickell (1686–1740), tells how a cunning fairy, Milkah, keeps a kidnapped prince of England, Albion, from growing:

In real life **daisies** were used to cure practically anything, from backaches and bruises to sore eyes.

For skilful Milkah spar'd not to employ
Her utmost art to rear the princely boy;
Each supple limb she swath'd,   [wrapped]
   and tender bone,
And to the Elfin standard kept him down;
She robb'd dwarf-elders of their
   fragrant fruit,   [dwarf-elder berries]
And fed him early with the daisy's root,
Whence through his veins
   the powerful juices ran,
And form'd in beauteous miniature
   the man.

Flux-weed, an ingredient in Polyjuice Potion, was said in real life to heal broken bones.

Albion grows to just twelve inches tall, though he is a giant to the ten-inch-tall fairies.

Knotgrass. This plant is a key ingredient in Polyjuice Potion, which changes a person into someone else. In real life it was often used as a remedy. Knotgrass juice supposedly stops nosebleeds, says Culpeper; if the plant is boiled in wine 'it is profitable to those that are stung or bitten by venomous creatures . . . [and] kills worms in the belly or stomach'. Made into tea it had even more uses.

Folklore offers another use, related to the shape-shifting power of Polyjuice Potion: like daisy-roots, it supposedly stunts growth. In Shakespeare's *A Midsummer Night's Dream*, a young man rudely tells a woman who is self-conscious about being short: 'Get you gone, you dwarf; you minimus, of hindering knot-grass made'. Shakespeare's friends and fellow playwrights Francis Beaumont (1584–1616) and John Fletcher (1579–1625) make a similar reference in one of their plays: 'We want a boy . . . kept under for a year with milk and knotgrass'.

It's a fair bet that Harry would struggle in Potions class even if someone nicer than Professor Snape were teaching it. It's hard

The seed of some **ferns** is so small it can't easily be seen by the naked eye, leading to the notion that carrying a pouch of it could make a person invisible.

See
Cauldrons
Herbology

enough to keep track of the ingredients, much less the recipes. And it turns out there's history to learn, also – not Harry's favourite subject. But Snape's potions – at least those he teaches in Hogwarts' first few years – aren't impossible to master. Muggles have done it for years.

What Makes Harry a Universal Hero?

THE DETAILS OF HARRY'S LIFE ARE WELL known to his fans. Some of them have even deduced facts J. K. Rowling leaves out, such the year he was born (see sidebar).

HARRY THE HERO

But if we understand Harry's character deeply, it is not solely because of the facts. It seems that Harry, for all his unique qualities, is a very familiar hero. He is, from the very start of *Stone*, what readers might call a legendary Lost Prince or Hidden Monarch – just like Oedipus, Moses, King Arthur, and countless others in every culture. He never knew he was a wizard – or even that the magical world existed – before receiving the letter inviting him to Hogwarts.

Making him even more familiar, he is, at least by the Dursleys' strange standards, an Ugly Duckling. They think everything about

Harry's **birthday** is 31 July 1980. The newspaper story about the Gringott's Bank robbery in *Stone* tells the day. The year is revealed by Nearly Headless Nick's 500th Deathday in *Chamber*. It takes place in 1992, and Harry is twelve. J. K. Rowling's birthday is also 31 July – but 1966.

him is odd. So they treat him as Cinderella was treated, imprisoning him in a world far less interesting than his birthright, forcing him to sleep under stairs when a four-poster bed awaits him at Hogwarts, and feeding him scraps, which makes him astounded at the abundance of Hogwarts feasts.

HOW HARRY SEES HIMSELF

Though Harry's introduction to the wizard world instantly offers the recognition he so desperately craves – everybody he meets has already heard of the great Harry Potter – he still feels self-doubt. The lightning scar is not the only mark Voldemort left. There was a deeper consequence to that battle. Some of Voldemort's psyche found its way into Harry. He worries about the question that stumped the Sorting Hat early in *Stone*: is he a Gryffindor, with the virtues that implies, or is he a Slytherin, susceptible to evil? In *Chamber*, Dumbledore explains a view of good and evil that has shades of grey, not just dark and light. The bit of Voldemort in Harry, he explains, simply makes him less conventional and more resourceful than the average Gryffindor. It also helps him understand Voldemort, which is an advantage. In future battles, this extra strength

Rowling has revealed only one thing about the final chapter of Harry's last adventure. The current version of it, kept in a secret place, ends with the word '**scar**'. Does that means the mark of Voldemort will finally disappear?

and knowledge – for example, the ability to speak with snakes that he gained from contact with Voldemort – will continue to help Harry.

BLOODLINES

Harry's mother, though a powerful witch, was Muggle-born. For those who care about bloodlines, like Draco Malfoy, Harry's status is inferior. But Harry seems, if anything, stronger for coming from mixed blood.

In fact, his conversations with Draco echo an incident in the childhood of another great British wizard, Merlin, in a legend recounted by the early historian Geoffrey of Monmouth: 'A sudden quarrel broke out between two of the lads, whose names were Merlin and Dinabutius. As they argued, Dinabutius said to Merlin: "Why do you try to compete with me, fathead? How can we two be equal in skill? I myself am of royal blood on both sides of my family. As for you, nobody knows who you are, for you never had a father!"'

But Merlin's nemesis, like Draco Malfoy, had a knack for prideful mistakes. His outburst attracted the attention of messengers for King Vortigern, who had been told to find a boy with no father. The young Merlin was brought to the king, and his career began that day.

Is it just a coincidence that Harry's parent's lived in **'Godric's Hollow'**? J. K. Rowling suggests not, but won't say more. Perhaps the Potter family home goes back to Godric Gryffindor, and Harry is the heir to Godric's legacy?

Harry's adventures also follow a familiar pattern. Scholar Joseph Campbell wrote at length about 'The Hero with a Thousand Faces', the common character central to cultures all over the world. From Odysseus of ancient Greek myth to Luke Skywalker of *Star Wars*, these heroes and their legends bear a striking similarity. Harry makes it a thousand and one.

Campbell summarized those stories this way: 'A hero ventures forth from the world of common day into a region of supernatural wonder. Fabulous forces are there encountered and decisive victory is won. The hero comes back from this mysterious adventure with the power to bestow boons on his fellow man.'

The hero's journey has three stages, which Campbell labels *Departure*, *Initiation* and *Return*. Within those stages are common themes. A glance at any of the books reveals evidence of the pattern:

I. Departure
The hero is called to adventure.
As Campbell describes it, the hero is first seen in our everyday world. He is beginning a new stage in life. A herald may arrive to announce that destiny has summoned the hero.

The very start of *Stone* fits this design. Harry is suffering a dreary life with the Dursleys when he learns a place is waiting for him at Hogwarts. Because the Dursleys have intercepted previous letters, Hagrid arrives to collect him.

Harry continues to spend summers with the Dursleys, so later books also begin with Harry in the ordinary world.

The hero may refuse the call to adventure. He may have any number of reasons, from everyday responsibilities to a selfish refusal to help others. But if he does, he will find that he has no choice in the matter.

Although Harry does not go through this step in *Stone*, he does in later books.

In *Chamber* he is annoyed by the public attention his earlier adventure has created, and craves anonymity. But his intrepid character makes it impossible for him to ignore the mysterious occurrences – which, as destiny would have it, are directed at him.

In *Goblet*, even though he decides not to trick the Goblet of Fire into accepting his entry for the Triwizard Tournament, it selects him anyway.

In *Phoenix*, he is summoned to appear before the Ministry of Magic to face criminal charges. He cannot avoid a conflict with the bureaucrats angered by his proclamation at the end of *Goblet* that Voldemort is back.

The hero meets a protector and guide who offers supernatural aid, often in the form of amulets.

This occurs again and again. In *Stone*, Hagrid has been one of Harry's protectors since birth. He was the wizard who first took Harry to the Dursleys when Harry was a baby. Soon after they meet again, when Harry is on his way to Hogwarts, they visit Diagon Alley, where Hagrid arranges for Harry to buy a wand and other wizarding supplies. As a birthday present, Hagrid also gives him an owl, Hedwig. As well, Dumbledore has been a protector and guide. In *Stone*, he gives Harry the invisibility cloak. And in *Azkaban*, Harry learns that Sirius has been protecting him.

The hero encounters the first threshold to a new world. The protector can only lead the hero to the threshold; the hero must cross it alone. He may first have to fight or outwit a guardian of the threshold who wants to prevent the crossing.

The climax of each of Harry's adventures begins with a solitary journey past a threshold.

In *Stone*, Ron can help Harry figure out the

right chess moves, and Hermione can help Harry figure out which potions will get him through the black flames; but only Harry can go into the last chamber, where he confronts Quirrell.

In *Chamber*, although he and Ron and Lockhart all travel down the drain to face the basilisk and save Ginny Weasley, Harry must make the final portion of the dangerous journey alone.

In *Phoenix*, Mr Weasley can lead Harry right to the door of the Wizengamot, but Harry must enter the room alone. The monsters in that room are as bad as those in any secret chamber.

In *Alice in Wonderland,* Alice also faces a challenging **chess match**.

The hero enters 'the Belly of the Whale', a phrase drawn from legends like the story of Jonah to signify being swallowed into the unknown.

Harry is in 'the Belly of the Whale' whether he plunges into the Chamber of Secrets, sneaks into Lupin's hideaway under the Whomping Willow in *Azkaban*, or faces the Wizengamot in the courtroom deep underground that Rowling refers to as a dungeon.

II. Initiation

The hero follows a road of trials. The setting is unfamiliar. The hero may encounter companions who assist him in these trials. Invisible forces may also aid him.

These themes reappear in each book. Harry receives new amulets each time, such as the invisibility cloak in *Stone* and the Marauder's Map in *Azkaban*. He learns how to call on forces such as his Patronus. In *Phoenix*, he receives training in Occlumency to prevent Voldemort from reading his mind.

Harry's **Patronus** appears as a stag, because that was his father's Animagus form.

The hero is abducted or must take a journey at night or by sea.

Harry is literally kidnapped in *Goblet* when he touches the Triwizard Cup, which has been turned into a portkey. In *Phoenix*, he feels as though he has been kidnapped while he sleeps.

The hero fights a symbolic dragon. He may suffer a ritual death, perhaps even dismemberment.

Harry battles a basilisk, Dementors, and, of course, the greatest symbolic dragon of all – Voldemort.

And it seems that in each adventure Harry suffers new, crippling injuries – for instance, he is literally dismembered in *Chamber*, when his arm breaks during the Quidditch match and his bones are accidentally removed with an incompetent spell.

The hero is recognized by or reunited with his father. He comes to understand this source of control over his life.

In every adventure Harry experiences a deeply touching moment of contact with his parents, such as when they appear in the Mirror of Erised in *Stone* and as ghost images released from Voldemort's wand in *Goblet*. He sees them again when he retrieves Snape's memory from the pensieve in *Phoenix*. That vision suddenly makes clear why Snape has hated him from the moment they met.

The hero becomes nearly divine. He has travelled past ignorance and fear.

Harry conquers fear in each adventure. Though he seems surprised to do so again and again, he has a sense, which grows after each confrontation with Voldemort, that the Dark Lord will not defeat him. As Dumbledore says at the end of *Goblet*, 'You have shouldered a grown wizard's burden and found yourself equal to it.' Rowling has Dumbledore make almost the same speech at the end of *Harry Potter and the Order of the Phoenix*: 'You rose magnificently to the challenge that faced you . . . You fought a man's fight.' Dumble-dore is almost unspeakably proud.

The hero receives 'the ultimate boon', the goal of his quest. It may be an elixir of life. It may be different from the hero's original goal because he is wiser.

A commoner may be revealed to be the descendant of a great hero upon receiving the hero's **sword**. King Arthur pulled Excalibur from a stone; in a Norse saga, Sigmund is given a sword by the god Odin, who later gives it to Sigmund's son. Harry pulls Godric Gryffindor's sword from the Sorting Hat. Could it be?

In *Stone*, the Mirror of Erised places 'the ultimate boon' – which in fact does make an elixir of life – right in his pocket.

In *Chamber*, he defeats the monster that has lived underneath Hogwarts for decades, saving Ginny Weasley (and countless other students who might have become the basilisk's victims).

In *Azkaban*, he 'finds' the prize all the wizards are seeking: Sirius Black. But having learned the truth about Black, he finds a way to spare him an apparently inevitable death sentence – just as if he had given him an elixir of life.

In *Goblet*, the goal is obvious: the victory in the Triwizard Tournament. But what Harry discovers is much deeper. He fights Voldemort wand-to-wand, and escapes death again – this time by virtue of his own skills. He begins to realize just how powerful a wizard he is.

In *Phoenix*, he learns about the powerful prophecy made about him as a baby, finally learning why Voldemort wants to kill him.

III. Return

The hero takes a 'magic flight' back to his original world. He may be rescued by magical forces. One of his original protectors may aid him. A person or thing from his original world may appear to bring him back.

Harry is miraculously saved in *Stone*, and travels back while still unconscious.

In *Chamber*, he is rescued by Fawkes. The phoenix brings the Sorting Hat to deliver Gryffindor's sword, then attacks the basilisk.

In *Goblet*, speaking to the image of Cedric Diggory released from Voldemort's wand, Harry makes a solemn commitment to return Diggory's body to Hogwarts. He is then transported back by the Triwizard Cup, which has been turned into a portkey.

In *Phoenix*, Dumbledore turns the head of the wizard from the Ministry's statue into a portkey, then hands it to Harry to magically speed him back to Hogwarts.

The hero crosses the return threshold. He may have difficulty adjusting to his original life, where people will not fully comprehend his experience.

After each school year he must return to the Dursley home on Privet Drive, where understanding is impossible. Even other wizards have trouble comprehending, as J. K. Rowling describes at the end of *Harry Potter and the Prisoner of Azkaban*: 'Nobody at Hogwarts now knew the truth of what had happened . . . As the end of term approached, Harry heard many different theories about what had really happened, but none of them came close to the truth.' Rowling revisits the same idea at the end of *Harry Potter and the Order of the Phoenix*: 'Perhaps the reason he wanted to be alone was because he felt isolated from everybody since his talk with Dumbledore. An invisible barrier separated him from the rest of the world.'

The hero becomes master of two worlds: the everyday world, which represents his material existence; and the magical world, which signifies his inner self.

Simply being in the presence of Voldemort is the worst nightmare of most wizards. But Harry has been there often, seeing things no other wizard has seen. These encounters have made him aware of a part of his psyche that other wizards never consider. One can be sure that eventually – even if he is doubtful – these experiences will help him become a greater wizard than even Dumbledore. (No doubt Dumbledore is aware of this, and pleased by it.)

The hero has won the freedom to live. He has conquered the fears that prevent him from living fully.

Fear, we are told, is Harry's greatest enemy – even greater than Voldemort. Professor Lupin did not let Harry practise fighting the boggart because he did not want an image of Voldemort flying through Hogwarts. But Harry tells him, 'I didn't think of Voldemort . . . I remembered those Dementors.' Lupin is impressed by Harry's insight. 'That suggests that what you fear most of all is fear. Very wise, Harry.' (*Harry Potter and the Prisoner of Azkaban* by J. K. Rowling)

ACTING THE HERO

In *Harry Potter and the Order of the Phoenix*, Rowling herself pokes a bit of fun at the repetition of these ideas: Ron challenges Harry about 'acting the hero' and Hermione asks if he might have a 'saving-people thing'. But Rowling does not follow a step-by-step diagram. These patterns appear in each of

See also:
Dumbledore
Voldemort

Rowling's books, as they have in mythology and folklore for centuries, because the quest of heroes stays the same. To battle the dark forces in the world, heroes must face the dark forces within, and rediscover in each adventure that they are worthy of victory. We understand Harry because, as Campbell says, 'every one of us shares the supreme ordeal.'

Why Are Runes Carved on the Pensieve?

Runes

DUMBLEDORE HAS SO MANY MEMORIES HE stores some in a pensieve, 'a shallow stone basin' with 'odd carvings around the edge'. (*Harry Potter and the Goblet of Fire*) J. K. Rowling created the name from the French word *penser* ('to think') and *sieve*, which is a tool used to strain liquids and separate out desired things.

Harry recognizes some of the carvings as runes. So what are runes, and why would they belong on a pensieve?

Runes were the first alphabet of the tribes of northern Europe, used in Britain, Scandinavia and Iceland. They appeared about the third century AD and endured more than a millennium. The first six letters were f, u, th, a, r and k, so the alphabet is sometimes called 'futhark'.

Viking **runes** carved on a rock.

Rûn is Gaelic for 'secret', and *helrûn* means 'divination', suggesting that the alphabet was

Runes appear often in J. R. R. Tolkien's *The Lord of the Rings*. The all-important ring mentioned in the title is engraved with a runic message. Tolkien, who loved creating new words as much as J. K. Rowling does, created an entire runic alphabet and language.

used in magic rituals. They are said to come from the gods themselves. Odin hanged himself for nine days from Yggdrasil, the great ash tree that holds earth, heaven and hell, to earn knowledge of the runes. Odin's sacrifice to gain knowledge for humankind symbolizes how greatly learning was valued. In fact, when runes were first used there was little distinction between scholars and wizards. Runes were sometimes used for divination, and in recent years this practice has become popular again. Their symbols are read the way some fortune-tellers read tarot cards.

In *Pheonix*, Hermione takes Ancient Runes and worries that she confused two of them, *ehwaz* and *eihwaz*, on her exam. She did. The definitions Rowling mentions are actually used by people who cast runes to tell fortunes: *ehwaz* signifies partnership and *eihwaz* signifies defence.

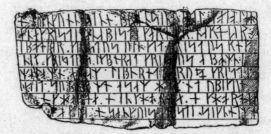

A tablet carved with runes, from about AD 1000.

Why Does the Sphinx Ask Harry a Question?

DURING THE THIRD TASK OF THE Triwizard Tournament, as he nears the centre of the maze, Harry meets a Sphinx – 'an extraordinary creature', part lion and part woman, with 'long, almond-shaped eyes'. She tells him, 'You are very near your goal. The quickest way is past me.' (*Harry Potter and the Goblet of Fire* by J. K. Rowling) But instead of fighting her, as he would a dragon, he must answer a question.

The face on the Great Sphinx at Giza was actually modelled on a king of Egypt.

The Sphinx is a creature from Egyptian mythology. The huge stone sculpture of the Great Sphinx in the Egyptian desert at Giza, built about 2500 BC, is evidence of the creature's ancient origins and importance. Thousands of smaller Sphinxes were built around Egypt, occasionally with heads modelled on birds of prey.

In the thousand years after the Great Sphinx was built, the legends of the creature moved to Greece. There it was described as having a female body and wings. The Sphinx Harry meets is the Greek version.

The Sphinx's strange form and enigmatic manner make it the very symbol of mystery. William Shakespeare once asked, 'is not Love . . . subtle as a Sphinx?' *Love's Labours Lost* (Act IV, scene iii).

THE SPHINX OF THEBES

A particular Sphinx of Greek legend is especially well known. It was sent by the goddess Hera to punish Laius, the king of Thebes, who had kidnapped a young man. That Sphinx challenged travellers on the road to Thebes with a three-part riddle similar to the one Harry was asked to solve:

> *What animal goes on four feet in*
> *   the morning,*
> *Two at noon,*
> *And three in the evening?*

Any traveller was permitted to turn back without answering; but the Sphinx killed anyone who answered incorrectly.

One day it was approached by a young man named Oedipus. He happened to be Laius's son and heir. (But, like Harry, he was unaware of his noble origins.) Oedipus displayed his exceptional qualities by answering the riddle correctly: 'Man creeps on hands and knees in childhood, walks upright in adulthood, and in old age uses a cane.' Having been bested, the Sphinx killed herself.

Another type of sphinx, with the head of a ram, was known as the **Criosphinx**. (*Krios* is ancient Greek for 'ram'.)

The Sphinx questions Oedipus.

In another version of the story, the questioner is not a creature but Oedipus's sister. They don't know each other because Oedipus had left home at an early age. But she has been told about a secret prophecy that Laius's son would return to Thebes, so it was her habit to question all men who came to the city. Oedipus had been told of the prophecy in a dream, so he answered her questions correctly and claimed the kingdom.

See also:

Beasts

Centaurs

Fluffy

Mazes

How Do You Scare a Spider?

ALL SORTS OF SPIDERS – SOME ORDINARY, some unusual – live near Hogwarts. Most of them are common and harmless. A few, like Aragog, Mosag and their children, are huge, intelligent, and gifted with speech.

ARAGOG'S NAME

The source of Aragog's name is the same as the source of 'arachnid', the scientific name for spiders. They both come from a mythical woman, Arachne, who was especially gifted in spinning and weaving. Being a bit too proud,

Arachne challenged Athena, Greek goddess of handicrafts, to a contest. Arachne beat Athena, but the goddess was so annoyed that she turned Arachne into a spider, forcing her to weave only webs. The names Aragog and Mosag also echo the names of the giants Gog and Magog. As well, *mosag* is a Gaelic word meaning 'dirty woman'. And in what is probably just a nice coincidence, it's also nearly an anagram of 'gossamer' – something light as air, like a spider's web.

The goddess
Athena

MAN-EATERS

In *Chamber*, Aragog seems perfectly willing to let his children eat Ron and Harry. He is following a long tradition. Many authors have enjoyed creating man-eating monsters out of spiders. By comparison, J. K. Rowling's spiders, though perfectly happy to eat humans, seem more understanding than most. They're much kinder than Shelob, the one created by J. R. R. Tolkien in *The Lord of the Rings*, who ate any humans or elves unlucky enough to stumble into her cave and thought of little except her next meal.

THE USEFULNESS OF SPIDERS

Evil spiders are common; but there have been many instances of spiders helping humans. In the early 1300s, Robert the Bruce, King of Scotland, was inspired to resist the English one last time when he saw a spider tenaciously struggling to build a web. He and his followers went on to win their full independence. As a result, a legend arose that no kinsman of Bruce could kill a spider!

Often spiders enjoy powerful knowledge. Native Americans tell stories of Iktomi, a trickster spirit, who imparted his wisdom to a Lakota while spinning a web. There is both good and bad in the world, Iktomi explained. Wisdom is heeding the good while letting the bad pass by. He told his student to use the web to catch the good while letting the evil pass through the hole at the centre. Thus was created the custom of hanging dreamcatchers, rings strung with webbing, over a bed to catch good dreams. Among the legends of the Pacific Islands is the story of a spider called Areop-Enap, who existed at the beginning of time, when there was only the sea and himself. Then Areop-Enap created all the other things in the world – the moon, the sun and humankind. The legends of Ghana include another trickster spider-god, Anansi, who creates the world and then delights in playing jokes on humans.

Aragog and his family are good examples of what seem to be important rules in Harry's world: appearances can be deceiving; and most creatures, like humans, tend to treat others only as badly as they've been treated.

It makes sense that underneath the ugliness and anger of Aragog is a feeling creature that can be good rather than evil. In fact, he gives Harry an important clue to the mystery of the Chamber of Secrets. For a time, Aragog was mistakenly believed to be the monster set free from the chamber fifty years before Harry's adventure. But that monster, says Aragog in Rowling's *Harry Potter and the Chamber of Secrets*, was actually 'an ancient creature we spiders fear above all others'. Harry later learns Aragog is referring to the basilisk; and when he sees spiders fleeing Hogwarts he knows the great snake is loose.

See also:
Basilisk

Why Do Trolls Stink?

TROLLS ARE A RACE OF OGRES – UNPLEASANT in both appearance and personality. Professor Quirrell, who later claims 'a special gift with trolls', secretly lets a mountain troll into Hogwarts: 'It was a horrible sight. Twelve feet tall, its skin was a dull, granite grey, its great lumpy body like a boulder with its small bald head perched on top like a coconut. It had short legs thick as tree trunks with flat, horny feet. The smell coming from it was incredible.' (*Harry Potter and the Philosopher's Stone* by J. K. Rowling)

Legends of trolls originated in Scandinavia, where the creatures alarmed residents of the countryside with their size and magical ability. According to some legends they lived in castles; other stories had them living in underground palaces. They only came out at night, and could be turned into stone by sunlight.

As Scandinavians moved to Britain, trolls

Magical creatures expert Carol Rose says that in Norway, female trolls were beautiful.

were said to have tagged along, making their homes under bridges. That may explain why they reek of sewer water.

Their bad reputation among humans is based on a variety of legends. They dislike the noise humans make, so they are often cranky; they snatch women and children; some of them are cannibals. In *Peer Gynt*, a famous play by Norwegian author Henrik Ibsen, the title character lightheartedly acts like a troll, warning: 'I'll come to your bedside at midnight tonight. If you should hear someone hissing and spitting, you mustn't imagine it's only the cat. It's me, lass! I'll drain out your blood in a cup; and your little sister, I'll eat her up.'

Perhaps trolls, like giants, are judged unfairly. Later in Ibsen's play, Peer Gynt actually meets a troll, who tells him, 'We troll-folk, my son, are less black than we're painted.' It's hard to believe that trolls are actually kind, though they may be no worse than humans. At one point Gynt's friend asks him, 'What difference is there 'twixt trolls and men?' Gynt replies, 'No difference at all, as it seems to me. Big trolls would roast you and small trolls would claw you; with us it would be likewise, if only men dared.'

Certain large rocks in the British north lands are said to be trolls who stayed out until daybreak.

See also:
Goblins

Why Should Wizards Never Be Inquisitors?

DOLORES UMBRIDGE'S TITLE, 'HIGH Inquisitor', should send chills down the spine of both wizards and Muggles. It comes from a long, bloody period in history that affected witches and laypeople alike, and which seems to reappear in different forms in almost every era – including our own, as J. K. Rowling suggests with some clever comments.

ASK ME NO QUESTIONS . . .

'High Inquisitor' is meant to bring to mind the Inquisition, a series of unfair trials in Europe that lasted hundreds of years. The goal of each Inquisition was to make people believe what the authorities wanted them to believe. If you disagreed with the government or church – often they were same thing – you might die.

The authorities took such extreme action for the same reason they always have: fear of

'Dolores' comes from the Latin word for 'pain.' In English, 'dolor' means 'grief' or 'sorrow.' **'Umbridge'** is a play on 'umbrage', which means 'resentment.' (As in: Dolores Umbridge takes umbrage when you challenge her, so you're going to be very sorry now.)

losing their authority. (Think about it: why have trials for people you believe are doomed to eternal damnation?) This fear led the Inquisitors to abuse their power. Accusations could be made secretly, so people lied to make trouble for enemies. Trials were also secret. The accused person did not have the right to a lawyer. Most shocking but very common was torture. Many confessions were forced.

The first 'Inquisition' began in the early 1200s in France, Germany, and Spain. Pope Gregory IX named an 'Inquisitor-General' to put an end to doubts about the church's control of how people could worship. The practice lasted centuries. Its intensity changed with the

A medieval woodcut of Jews about to face death in the Inquisition.

mood of the times – for example it got new life when the Church tried to stop the spread of Protestantism in the mid-1500s.

A separate Inquisition began in Spain in 1478 and lasted in various forms until the 1820s. It was especially fierce. The first Grand Inquisitor was the famous Tomás de Torquemada (1420–1498). His stated goal was no different than Voldemort's: he wanted only people with *sangre limpia* – 'pure blood', defined by him as white and Christian – to live in Spain. He executed somewhere between 2,000 and 10,000 people in just twenty years, with perhaps another 10,000 punished in other ways. He hounded thousands of Jews, Muslims, and others until they left Spain, and had Jews expelled by law in 1492.

Frenchman Nicholas Rémy (1530–1616) claimed to have personally directed the execution of nine hundred witches in a single decade.

'THE BURNING TIMES'

Sorcerers and witches were often a special target of the Inquisitions. By the 1300s, accusations of witchcraft were common and often led to executions. The Church had decided that magic was the work of the Devil, and that a sorcerer must have made a deal with Devil to gain magical knowledge and skill.

Ignoring or laughing at this nonsense only made things worse. One French monk and judge, Jean Bodin (1529–1596), came up with the rule that anyone who denied the existence of witches must also be a witch.

Bodin was a fan of torture and harsh punishment. 'The country which shall tolerate this [witchcraft]', he wrote, 'will be scourged

Burning witches was favoured for its cruelty and because it supposedly purifed the soul. But it was a lot of trouble and very expensive. Many witches were hanged instead.

with pestilences, famines and wars.' But people who 'take vengeance on the witches will be blessed by God'.

A witch known for kind acts such as healing was no safer than someone accused of using magic for evil. Bodin wrote: 'Even if the witch has never killed or done evil to a man, or beasts, or fruits, and even if he has always cured bewitched people, or driven away tempests, it is because he has renounced God and treated with [made a deal with] Satan that he deserves to be burned alive. Even no more than an obligation to the Devil, which means denying God, deserves the most cruel death imaginable.'

Thanks to bloodthirsty inquisitors like Bodin, the times when witch-hunts were at their worst were known as 'burning times'. Perhaps two hundred thousand people accused of being witches were killed in Europe and America from the time of the first Inquisition until the nineteenth century, when religion became more moderate.

Most of the victims did not practice magic at all. They were simply victims of angry neighbours and relatives, or greedy prosecutors who wanted to take their property. Sometimes they were picked just because they seemed odd. For example, a woman who did not marry or take part in the social activities was more likely to be called a witch than one who had family ties or a high place in society.

This sad fact is something that scholars see in all cultures, especially when the economy is

Jean Bodin's book *The Demonomania of Witches* (1580), which claimed to explain all the evil practices of magic, was a strong influence on prosecutors. Ironically, all of his other books, which explained his political theories, were denounced by the Inquisition.

bad or a natural disaster has occurred: humans seek someone weak to sacrifice, as if that will win the goodwill of the gods or God and restore a natural order to the world. The 1692 witch trials in Salem, Massachusetts, began after the colonists had suffered in wars with Native Americans, which made them wonder if their religious settlement still enjoyed God's favour. This pattern continues today, sometimes with violence and other times with more subtlety.

MODERN WITCH-HUNTS

J. K. Rowling's High Inquisitor is more than a reference to the Inquisition. The term 'witch-hunt' is used in modern times too, to describe the way governments and other institutions unfairly claim certain vulnerable people are guilty of hurting society as a whole, often for something vague and unproven. In the 1950s, it was common for Western nations to conduct 'witch-hunts' of people who believed in communism, a belief the government said automatically made those people dangerous to others. Communist countries did the same, hunting for people who didn't support their governments. In many cases the government charges were nonsense. And even those who

Witchcraft was illegal in Britain until 1951, when the last laws against it were replaced with the Fraudulent Medium Act. The new law suggested that witches weren't dangerous but were trying to fool people into paying for magical help.

didn't support the authorities were rarely any sort of threat.

This is exactly what happens to Harry at the Wizengamot in *Phoenix*. Having said in *Goblet* that Voldemort has returned, and that some Dementors are under Voldemort's control, he has challenged the official position of the Ministry of Magic; so in *Phoenix* Cornelius Fudge and Dolores Umbridge make him stand trial to silence him. They even attempt to keep him from having the help of Dumbledore's counsel just as in the old days of the Inquisition, and as sometimes happens today when governments go too far. The connection to today is what Rowling wants us to see. When Dolores Umbridge waves the list of students in Dumbledore's Army she's doing exactly what one of the most famous witch-hunters of the twentieth century did to attack his enemies. U.S. Senator Joseph McCarthy is remembered for waving a piece of paper that supposedly showed top government officials were traitors. The list was phoney; but he was discredited only after he had ruined many lives by forcing people to face a U.S. government inquisition that lasted years.

Dolores Umbridge uses another common trick against Griselda Marchbanks. When

The **Salem witch-hunts** began when two young girls accused a servant and two other women of witchcraft. In time the hysteria spread to other towns and the girls travelled as 'experts'. Twenty-five people were dead before the mob violence ended.

Marchbanks protests the Hogwarts inquisition, Umbridge spreads lies that Marchbanks is working with goblins who want to overthrow the wizards. She is trying to assassinate Marchbank's character by appealing to the other wizards' fear of goblins. That's a trick used all the time, from medieval inquisitions to modern politics.

IS ALL FAIR IN LOVE AND WAR?

See also:
Fortescue
Order of the
   Phoenix
Death Eaters

Dolores Umbridge and Cornelius Fudge have plenty of excuses for what they do. That's always the way. Inquisitions have always been tolerated or excused by people who refuse to question the perfection of their religion or their nation. J. K. Rowling isn't one of those people. For her, nothing is more important than having the courage to think for ourselves. Umbridge, who for all her faults is still a witch, should have shuddered at the title of High Inquisitor of Hogwarts. Any wizard should know better.

How Do You Catch a Unicorn?

FEW MAGICAL CREATURES HAVE STRUCK the human imagination as deeply as the elegant unicorn. Even in Harry's wizard world, with so many wondrous beasts, the unicorn is a symbol of the sacred. In *Harry Potter and the Philosopher's Stone*, J. K. Rowling says unicorns have 'silvery' blood; and in *Harry Potter and the Goblet of Fire* she describes unicorn

239

foals that are 'pure gold', adding that their coats will turn silver around age two, and 'go pure white' when the unicorns mature.

The Unicorn in Lewis Carroll's *Through the Looking-glass*, like everything else in the story, is the opposite of what you would expect: He is anything but peaceful – in fact he casually sticks other creatures with his horn. And when he is introduced to Alice, he is the one surprised to meet a human: 'I always thought they were fabulous [mythical] monsters! . . . Is it alive?'

Ancient Unicorns

Unicorns appear in the ancient art and myths of Mesopotamia, China and India. The Roman naturalist Pliny, relying on reports he had heard, listed a few varieties of unicorns, each with horns of about two cubits (three feet) on its forehead: one, 'a most swift beast', could mimic a human voice; another could move its horn at will, to use as a weapon; and yet another had skin that 'cannot be pierced'.

A traveller from the early 1500s saw two unicorns at the temple of Mecca:

> The elder is formed like a colt of thirty months old, and he has a horn in the forehead, which horn is about as long as three arms. The other unicorn is like a colt of one year old, and he has a horn of about one foot long. The colour of the said animal resembles that of a dark bay horse, and his head resembles that of a stag; his neck is not very long, and he has some thin and short hair which hangs on one side; his legs are slender and lean like

those of a goat; the foot is a little cloven in the fore part, and long and goatlike, and there are some hairs on the hind part of the said legs. Truly this monster must be a very fierce and solitary animal. These two animals were presented to the Sultan of Mecca as the finest things that could be found in the world at the present day, and as the richest treasure ever sent by a king of Ethiopia, that is, by a Moorish king. He made this present in order to secure an alliance with the said Sultan of Mecca.

Pliny reported that the unicorn can 'never become tamed'. William Shakespeare referred to the same elusive nature: 'Time's glory is to calm contending kings, to unmask falsehood and bring truth to light . . . to tame the unicorn and lion wild.'

Other writers suggest the trick is to bait the unicorn with a young virgin – and although this method has never been successfully employed, it fits with the unicorn's role as a symbol of purity and chastity. Many medieval tapestries portray scenes of unicorns to convey the power of sacred devotion. The Old Testament refers to unicorns several times: 'God brought them out of Egypt; he hath as it

Chinese legend also mentions a sacred unicorn with a deer's body, ox's tail, and horse's hooves. Its coat is five different colours. It lives 1000 years.

were the strength of the unicorn' (Numbers 23:22); 'His horns are like the horns of unicorns: with them he shall push the people together to the ends of the earth' (Deuteronomy 33:17); 'My horn shall thou exalt like the horn of a unicorn' (Psalms 92:10); 'Will the unicorn be willing to serve thee, or abide in thy crib?' (Job 39:9). These references, to some scholars, indicate that the unicorn is actually a symbol of Christ. Others disagree. The word in the original text would be better translated as 'wild ox'. Perhaps the translators of the King James Version (1611)

Unicorn appearing on a family crest.

were influenced by the knowledge that their patron, King James I of Britain, considered the unicorn his emblem.

HORN OF PLENTY

The unicorn's ability to save one's body as well as one's soul has always been a part of its legend. Ctesias, a Greek physician in the employ of the ruler of Persia around 400 BC, wrote one of the first accounts of the creature:

> There are in India certain wild asses which are as large as horses, and larger. Their bodies are white, their heads dark red, and their eyes dark blue. They have a horn on the forehead that is about a foot and a half in length. The dust filed from this horn is administered in a potion as a protection against deadly drugs. The base of this horn, for some two hands'-breadth above the brow, is pure white; the upper part is sharp and of a vivid crimson; and the remainder, or middle portion, is black. Those who drink out of these horns, made into drinking vessels, are not subject, they say, to convulsions or to the holy disease [epilepsy]. Indeed, they are immune even to poisons if either before

The unicorn was the emblem of Scotland's royal House of Stuart. James VI of Scotland, upon becoming **James I** of Britain in 1603, added the unicorn to the British coat of arms, opposite the English lion. It is said to represent Scotland's independent spirit. In *The Faerie Queen* (1596) Edmund Spenser mentions the 'Lion, whose imperial power a proud rebellious Unicorn defies.'

or after swallowing such, they drink wine, water, or anything else from these beakers.

These medicinal qualities, so important to the critically ill like Voldemort – who kills a unicorn to drink its life-sustaining blood – once made the unicorn an object of hunters. (Of course those hunters were frustrated.)

EVERYTHING OLD IS NEW AGAIN

Close readers of Rowling's *Fantastic Beasts and Where to Find Them* may have noticed a similar healing power is mentioned for the magical creature called the Re'em. Its blood, although hard to come by, 'gives the drinker immense strength'. That's a very sly connection by Rowling. The Hebrew word that the translators of the King James Bible turned into 'unicorn' is *re'em*. Rowling's animal combines the original Hebrew meaning with qualities later associated with unicorns. Like the biblical animals, Rowling's Re'em are 'giant oxen.' Like unicorns, they are 'extremely rare' and capturing them is difficult.

In modern Hebrew, *re'em* refers to a horned gazelle, says Gili Bar-Hillel, the translator of Rowling's works into Hebrew, who helped uncover the biblical source. No doubt that animal inspired some early descriptions of unicorns.

See also:

Centaurs

Forest

What Makes Veela Angry?

VEELA, SEDUCTIVE NATURE SPIRITS WHO first appear in *Goblet*, originate in legends of Central Europe. They are beautiful young women – or appear to be such. In some stories they are said to be ghosts of unbaptized women whose souls cannot leave earth. Their beauty is astonishing and can make men act foolishly. They have long hair, so fair it seems white.

THE DARK SIDE OF VEELA

Veela can be quite jealous. A famous Serbian tale, 'Prince Marko and the Veela', tells of an encounter with the veela Ravioyla:

> Two brothers, Duke Milosh and Kralyevich Marko, rode side by side over magnificent Miroch Mountain. As the sun rose, Marko fell asleep, then awoke with a start.

Veela are the nymphs and dryads – the nature spirits – of Greek mythology, made into local spirits.

'Milosh,' he said, 'I cannot stay awake. Sing to me to keep from sleeping.'

Duke Milosh answered, 'Oh, Kralyevich Marko, I cannot sing to you. Last night I drank with the veela Ravioyla, and drank too much and sang too loudly and too well, and the veela warned me that if I sing on her mountain she will shoot her arrows into me.'

Kralyevich Marko replied, 'Brother,

Kralyevich Marko is named for a real leader of Serbia, but the real Marko is not believed to have been heroic or even particularly interesting. He seems to have received the credit for the the deeds of others, and of course to have benefited from the skills of storytellers.

you cannot be afraid of a veela. I am Kral-yevich Marko. With my golden battle-axe, we are both safe.' So Milosh sang, telling a story of kings and kingdoms and the glory of our country.

Marko listened, but the song did not keep sleep away. Soon he was dreaming again.

The veela Ravioyla heard Milosh, and she sang back to him in a beautiful voice. But Milosh answered her in a voice that was even finer, and she became angry as she had before. She flew to Miroch Mountain, and expertly drew two arrows at once in her bow. One hit Milosh in the throat, silencing him. The other hit his heart.

Both horses stopped, and Marko awoke. With great effort Milosh was able to speak, but only in a dying whisper. He said to Marko, 'Brother! Veela Ravioyla has shot me because I sang on Miroch Mountain.'

It was said that a veela in the form of a particular fairy visited mothers on the seventh night after the birth of a baby to tell the mother the baby's destiny.

Veela are also gifted in the healing arts, with a special knowledge of natural remedies. In the story above, the veela Ravioyla heals Milosh and tells other veela not to bother the men. In fact, veela tend to be kind to humans – and are known to marry mortal men.

See also:

Cornish Pixies

What upsets veela most is having their ritual dances disturbed. If that occurs, they may become fiercely angry. As spirits of the wind, veela can invoke whirlwinds and storms as they did during the Quidditch World Cup.

What Kind of Nightmares Created Voldemort?

NOTHING BRINGS OUT A GREAT HERO AS much as a great villain. Lord Voldemort – the half-Muggle born as Thomas Marvolo Riddle – fits the bill. It is no surprise that wizards call him the Dark Lord. That name describes a whole category of literary villains with whom Voldemort has much in common.

Critics John Clute and John Grant note a few characteristics that make a classic Dark Lord:

- A Dark Lord 'has often been already defeated but not destroyed aeons before'.
- He 'aspires to be the Prince of this world'.
- He is an 'abstract force', less flesh and blood than supernatural energy.
- He represents 'thinning', the idea that 'before the written story started there was a diminishment' such as the chaos and death Voldemort caused before Harry was sent to live with the Dursleys.

In French, '**Voldemort**' can mean either 'fly from death' or 'steal from death.' Both refer to a desire for immortality. In legend, Death often appears as a shadowy demon who has the right to everyone's life at some time. To live forever is said to be cheating Death or stealing from him.

249

Voldemort's
many ties to
serpents
(Slytherin
House; the form
hidden under
Quirrell's turban
in *Stone*; the
snake Nagini in
Goblet; the
nightmares in
Phoenix) fit with
evil snake
symbols going
back even
before Satan
was described
as a snake in
the Bible. As
well, since
ancient times,
Voldemort's
goals of rebirth
immortality
have been
symbolized by a
snake in a
curled into a
circle.

- He is also a symbol of 'debasement', a moral collapse, often as a result of a questionable bargain, such as the one struck by the many Death Eaters who sought to gain power through their alliance with Voldemort.
- He 'inflicts damage out of envy'.

By this reckoning, Voldemort is the very model of a Dark Lord. But for all his similarity to other villians, he also embodies J. K. Rowling's own definitions of evil. The first of those relates to society at large; the second is very personal.

LOVE THY NEIGHBOUR AS THYSELF

Voldemort is a creature of our times. Because his Muggle father abandoned his mother, he hates Muggles with what Rowling herself has called a 'racist' passion. She has said his obsession with 'pure' wizard bloodlines is like the Nazi's Aryan ideal or the Spanish Inquisition's goal of *sangre limpia* ('clean blood'). And she has directly connected Voldemort's mixed parentage to the odd case of Hitler, who fell far short of the ideal that he demanded others meet – or die. Voldemort, she explains, 'takes what he perceives to be a defect in himself, in other words, the non-purity of his blood, and he projects it onto others . . . He takes his own inferiority, and turns it back on other people and attempts to exterminate in them what he hates in himself.' That commentary is meant as much for today's society as for past injustices.

LUST FOR LIFE

The other aspect of Voldemort's evil comes from fragments of Rowling's own life. As he tells the Death Eaters who flock to him at the end of *Harry Potter and the Goblet of Fire*, 'You know my goal – to conquer death.'

This matter of immortality is never far from J. K. Rowling's imagination. The whole first book is devoted to Voldemort's quest for the Philosopher's Stone, an object that will allow him to create a new body and keep it alive forever.

This lust for eternal life is the essence of the Dark Lord's depravity. But is he really any different from the many people in our world who try to live as long they can? Dumbledore tells Harry, 'The Stone was really not such a wonderful thing. As much money and life as you could want! The two things most human beings would choose above all – the trouble is, humans do have a knack of choosing precisely those things that are worst for them.' (*Harry Potter and the Philosopher's Stone* by J. K. Rowling)

A Greek myth tells of **Tithonus**, prince of Troy, who was loved by Eos, goddess of the dawn. Eos asked Zeus to grant Tithonus immortality so they could stay together forever, but forgot to ask that he be given eternal youth. Tithonus lived long but kept aging until he was withered. Finally, out of mercy, he was changed into a grasshopper.

In every culture, immortality, though desirable, is against the laws of nature. Things must die so other things may be born. This is a constant theme in Rowling's work: accepting death and not fighting nature. She states it directly at the end of *Harry Potter and the Order of the Phoenix* when Voldemort says, 'There is nothing worse than death, Dumbledore!'; to which Dumbledore replies, 'You are quite wrong . . . Indeed, your failure to understand that there are things much worse than death has always been your greatest weakness.'

Immortality fascinates many writers, even those like Rowling who originally set out to write for young people. J. R. R. Tolkien was obsessed with the questions it raises. It is a strong element in Philip Pullman's novels. They and others, including Rowling, have acknowledged a common reason: the early loss of a parent. Philip Pullman's father died when Pullman was seven. Tolkien lost both parents as a child. When J. K. Rowling was just twelve her mother developed a severe illness that took her life when Rowling was only twenty-five. All of these authors wanted to fight nature. Writing Harry's story is one of Rowling's ways of coming to accept it. Like Harry, she has a personal reason for sharing Voldemort's desire but knows it must be fought.

Why Do Wizards Use Wands?

Without question, a wand is a wizard's most important tool. In Harry's world, they are made by combining parts of magical creatures – such as 'unicorn hairs, phoenix tail feathers, and the heart-strings of dragons' – with staffs of willow, mahogany, yew, oak, beech, maple and ebony. Each wand is not only matched to the person-ality of the individual, but actually chooses the wizard.

The **Druids** had different wands for each of their seven levels of priesthood.

Ancient Wands

It seems wizards have always used wands. These sticks – or in some cases large rods – focus magical strength.

Some anthropologists believe that Stone Age cave paintings showing people with sticks are meant to portray leaders of the clans hold-ing wands to attest to their power. That is only a guess, but strong evidence goes back at least

The Egyptian god Thoth was also pictured carrying an early version of a **caduceus**.

See also:
Druids
Egypt

to the time of ancient Egypt. Hieroglyphs show priests holding small rods. In Greek mythology, Hermes, messenger of the Greek gods, carried a special wand called a caduceus. This is a rod with wings, around which two serpents are twisted, meant to signify wisdom and healing powers. Physicians adopted it as their symbol hundreds of years ago and still use it today.

In the past some wizards have favoured wands made from the elder tree, which is considered especially magical. Those who practised dark magic often used cypress, which was associated with death. However, J. K. Rowling tells us Voldemort's wand is made of yew. That also makes sense. The yew has immense supernatural power. At one time the yew was one of the few evergreens in Britain, so it has become a symbol of both death and rebirth – the same immortality Voldemort desperately wants.

Are Any of the 'Famous Witches and Wizards' Real?

WHEN THEY FIRST TAKE THE HOGWARTS Express to school, Ron introduces Harry to the Famous Witches and Wizards trading cards that come with Chocolate Frogs. He mentions a few: Dumbledore, Merlin, Paracelsus, the Druidess Cliodna, Hengist of Woodcroft, Morgana, Ptolemy and Circe. Some of these wizards are actual historical figures. Others exist in legends going back hundreds of years.

AGRIPPA

Heinrich Cornelius Agrippa was a wizard during the Renaissance. Born Heinrich Cornelis near Cologne, Germany, in 1486, he took the name Agrippa in honour of the founder of his hometown.

He had a varied career, working as a doctor, lawyer, astrologer and faith healer. But he made enemies as quickly as friends and was

According to legend, says witchcraft expert Rosemary Ellen Guiley, toads are considered 'psychically sensitive' and can detect ghosts.

The magical philosopher Heinrich Cornelius **Agrippa**.

Agrippa was said to be accompanied by a spirit (a 'familiar') in the form of a **black dog**.

branded a sorcerer. In 1529, he published a book called *On Occult Philosophy*, combining ancient Hebrew and Greek texts to argue that the best way to know God was through magic. Because of his efforts he was forced to leave Germany. In France, where he had been a physician to the queen mother, he was jailed. He died in 1535.

Agrippa was one inspiration for Wolfgang Goethe's play *Faust*, in which a scholar makes a pact with the Devil – similar to the pact between Voldemort and his followers. His name also came to be the term for a special sorcerer's handbook cut into the shape of a person.

DRUIDESS CLIODNA

In Irish mythology, Cliodna has several roles, from goddess of beauty to ruler of the Land of Promise – the afterlife. She is also goddess of the sea. Some say she is symbolized at the seacoast by every ninth wave that breaks on shore. She has three enchanted birds that heal the sick.

PARACELSUS

Paracelsus, born in Switzerland in 1493, is considered a founder of modern chemistry and medicine. He began his career as a medical doctor, then turned to the study of magic, especially alchemy and divination. His reputation as a wizard and his role as a doctor are linked. Because he refused to limit himself to the traditional medical education of the time and developed his own successful treatments, he was deemed a sorcerer. But Paracelsus ignored his critics. 'The universities do not teach all things,' he said, 'so a doctor must seek out old wives, gypsies, sorcerers, wandering tribes, old robbers, and such outlaws and take lessons from them. A doctor must be a traveller. Knowledge is experience.'

Paracelsus developed several useful remedies. He also found the cause of silicosis, a

Paracelsus was born Philippus Aureolus Theophrastus Bombast von Hohenheim. The name he created for himself is immodest. It means 'beyond **Celsus**', referring to a noted physician of Ancient Rome.

The gifted doctor **Paracelsus**.

miner's disease that comes from inhaling metal vapours, which previously had been blamed on evil spirits. He helped stop an outbreak of the plague in 1534 with a form of vaccination.

Because of his attitude and accomplishments, other doctors disliked him. He spent almost a decade in academic exile – and was even forced to flee the city of Basel under cover of darkness in 1528. But by the time of his death in 1541 his reputation had improved greatly.

MORGANA

Morgana – sometimes known as Morgan Le Fay – was a powerful enchantress of British myth, especially gifted in the healing arts. Merlin was her tutor, and she is sometimes said to be the half-sister of King Arthur. She was often Arthur's rival, stealing his sword Excalibur and plotting his death. But she is also said have been the queen of Avalon, the fairyland where dying heroes are rewarded, and to have tried to heal Arthur there when he was wounded. According to some legends she lived in the Straits of Messina, off Italy. An unusual sea current in that area often draws phosphorescent creatures from the depths to the surface, creating the impression of strange lights or objects floating above the water. These are called Fata Morgana, from *fata*, the Italian word for fairy.

Some legends of Morgan le Fay come from tales of the ancient Greek sorceress, **Medea**. Both of them cast a spell on a cloak so that it would burst into flames and kill whoever wore it.

MERLIN

Merlin is considered one of the wisest wizards ever. A master sorcerer, he was said to have been an adviser to the British kings Vortigern, Uther Pendragon, and Arthur. Although he may have been based on a wizard who actually lived, the Merlin we know is a character created from fantastic legends. For instance, some say he arranged the huge stones at Stonehenge. Others say he was gifted in prophecy because he lived backwards, so he had already seen the future.

He is best known as King Arthur's mentor. In a noteworthy parallel, he hid the infant Arthur just as Dumbledore knew to hide Harry from Voldemort. The poet Alfred Lord Tennyson recounted that part of the legend in *Idylls of the King*:

'Merlin' is an English version of the Welsh name 'Myrddhin'. The stories now associated with Merlin draw on early tales of a wizard named **Ambrosius**, who supposedly lived in the sixth century. The historian Geoffrey of Monmouth, who relied heavily on legends, connected him to the tales of King Arthur.

> *By reason of the bitterness and grief*
> *That vext his mother, all before his time*
> *Was Arthur born, and all as soon as born*
> *Delivered at a secret postern-gate*
> *To Merlin, to be holden far apart*
> *Until his hour should come; because the lords*
> *Of that fierce day were as the lords of this,*
> *Wild beasts, and surely would have torn*
>   *the child*
> *Piecemeal among them, had they known;*
>   *for each*
> *But sought to rule for his own self and hand,*
> *And many hated Uther.*
> *Wherefore Merlin took the child,*
> *And gave him to Sir Anton, an old knight*
> *And ancient friend of Uther; and his wife*
> *Nursed the young prince, and reared him with*
>   *her own;*
> *And no man knew. And ever since the lords*
> *Have fought like wild beasts among themselves,*
> *So that the realm has gone to wrack.*

Merlin then became both Arthur's tutor and his counsellor, using his keen intelligence and innumerable acts of wizardry to help the young king fight Britain's enemies.

According to some stories, Merlin was tricked by the Lady of the Lake, whom he loved, into creating a magical column of air that she then used to imprison him for ever.

HENGIST OF WOODCROFT

This wizard either is or is named for a Saxon king of Britain. King Hengist and his brother Horsa – their names come from the German words for 'stallion' and 'horse' – arrived in Britain in AD 449 as mercenaries to help King Vortigern put down Pict and Scot rebels, but they eventually led a rebellion of their own. Hengist founded the kingdom of Kent.

The name Woodcroft may simply be one that J. K. Rowling spotted on a map and liked. In Peterborough, north of Kent, you can find a Woodcroft Castle, site of a grisly murder and an old ghost. In 1648 Dr Michael Hudson, chaplain to King Charles II, was killed there while battling Oliver Cromwell's troops. He is said to haunt the castle on the anniversary of his death. Sounds of the battle can be heard, as well as Hudson's cries for mercy.

Many Merlin stories are related to the legends of another early Welsh wizard, **Taliesen**. (See pages 24 and 53)

CIRCE

In Homer's ancient epic poem *The Odyssey*, Circe is a 'great and cunning goddess' who lives on an island. Odysseus's men, returning home after the Trojan War, stop at her island and become victims of this enchantress:

> When they reached Circe's house they found it built of cut stones, on a site that could be seen from far, in the middle of the forest. There were wild mountain wolves and lions prowling all round it – poor bewitched creatures whom she had tamed by her enchantments and drugged into subjection. Presently they reached the gates of the goddess's house, and as they stood there they could hear Circe within, singing most beautifully as she worked at her loom, making a web so fine, so soft, and of such dazzling colours as no one but a goddess could weave. They called her and she came down, unfastened the door, and bade them enter. They, thinking no evil, followed her.
>
>
>
> When she had got them into her house, she set them upon benches and seats and mixed them a drink with honey, but she drugged it with wicked poisons to make

them forget their homes, and when they had drunk she turned them into pigs by a stroke of her wand, and shut them up in her pigsties. They were like pigs – head, hair, and all – and they grunted just as pigs do; but their senses were the same as before, and they remembered everything.

Odysseus himself, having taken a special potion, resists Circe's charms and eventually frees his men.

ALBERIC GRUNNION

This name must have been inspired by the Alberich who is a powerful wizard in the German epic poem *Nibelungenlied* ('Song of the Nibelungen'). The poem is a mythical account of a historical event, the defeat by the Huns of the kingdom of Burgundy (now part of France) in AD 437. It has been the basis of many modern works, most importantly the Ring Cycle, a series of linked operas written in the nineteenth century by Richard Wagner. (When you see cartoons of opera singers wearing horned helmets, it is Wagner's Ring Cycle they're singing.)

In Wagner's version of the story, Alberich is king of the dwarfs, full of hate and ambition. When he discovers a hoard of gold

The name **Oberon**, which Shakespeare gave to the king of the fairies in *A Midsummer Night's Dream*, is an English form of Alberich.

guarded by unsuspecting maidens, he does not hesitate to swear off love for ever to win it. He uses the gold to make a ring that gives him great power. When the ring is stolen from him, he places a curse on it. Anyone else who wears it will suffer greatly. As the story goes on, others try to win the ring, paying the price for their desire.

One hero of the Ring Cycle wins a prize from Alberich that will be familiar to Harry Potter fans: an **invisibility cloak**.

See also:
Flamel

PTOLEMY

Claudius Ptolemaeus lived in Alexandria, Egypt, in the early part of the second century AD, where he was an astronomer and mathematician. He collected the world's knowledge of those fields into a book, eventually known as the *Almagest*, which influenced scholars for more than a thousand years. His most significant conclusion was that the Earth is the centre of the universe, and that all other celestial bodies revolve around it. This is known as the 'Ptolemaic system'. Although it was disproved in the 1500s by the astronomer Nicolaus Copernicus, Ptolemy's records of his observations of the heavens are still considered useful to scholars even if his conclusions are not.

Afterword

EVERY WRITER BEGINS AS A READER. AFTER DIGGING INTO her stories, one sees that J. K. Rowling must have been a terrific reader before she became a terrific writer. Just as impressive as her knowledge of myths and legends is her ability to make each one seem original and fresh.

In the bibliography of this book, as well as in the notes for each entry, you'll find suggestions of interesting books for further reading. The best place to start would certainly be a collection of Greek and Roman myths. If you want to dig deeper, an outstanding reference with many detailed reading suggestions is *The Encyclopedia of Fantasy* by John Clute and John Grant. If you're particularly interested in magical creatures, you'll like Carol Rose's encyclopedias, *Giants, Monsters and Dragons* and *Spirits, Fairies, Leprechauns and Goblins*. For information about wizards, good sources are Rosemary Ellen Guiley's *The Encyclopedia of Witches and Witchcraft* and Thomas Ogden's *Wizards and Sorcerers*. You might also want to find the wonderful *Dictionary of Imaginary Places*, by Alberto Manguel and Gianni Guadalupi. Many books explain people and creatures, but this may be the only one that brings together fantastic worlds. And as most readers already know, the Internet is full of information about the Harry Potter books. Some web addresses are listed in the bibliography.

Whatever you read while you're waiting for the next Harry Potter – or whatever you write – you're bound to uncover connections between Harry's world and the many magical worlds J. K. Rowling discovered before she created Harry. They stayed with her, and they'll stay with you too.

Acknowledgements

Many thanks to Sophie Gorell Barnes of MBA Literary Agents in London and Maja Nikolic of Writers House in New York for bringing this book to Clare Hulton and everyone at Puffin, including Francesca Dow, Amanda Li, Samantha Mackintosh, Jacqui McDonough, Elaine McQuade, Adele Minchin, Leah Thaxton, Julia Bruce, Nigel Hazle, Julie Howson, Shannon Park, and Penny Worms. My thanks to cover artist John Fordham.

I'd like to extend a special thanks to the publishers and translators of the book's international editions, whose insights have contributed greatly to this revision.

Thanks also to my parents and sisters, editors all, for their expert advice. Lena Tabori's aid was essential. Dr Christine D. Myers, Nora Freeberg, Andréa Swan, Evan Michael Williams and Gili Bar-Hillel offered sharp insights. Special thanks to Martin Berke, Laurie Brown, Max and Emily de La Bruyère, Linda Dudajek and Debbie Malicoat of R. R. Donnelley, Natasha Tabori Fried, Katie Kerr, Lyuba Konopasek, Miles Kronby, Arif Lalani, Laura Poole of Archer Editorial Services,

Edward Samuels, Stacy Schiff, Ben Shykind, John Ward of Ward & Olivo, Terry Wybel and Continental Sales, and Bristol Books in Wilmington, North Carolina.

The editor and publishers gratefully acknowledge the following for permission to reproduce copyright material in *The Magical Worlds of Harry Potter*.

The Sword in the Stone by T. H. White, HarperCollins Publishers Ltd, London
Latin for all Occasions by Henry Beard, HarperCollins Publishers Ltd, London
The Hero with a Thousand Faces by Joseph Campbell, © 1949 by Bollingen Foundation
A Wizard of Earthsea by Ursula K. Le Guin. Copyright © The Inter-vivos Trust for the Le Guin children
Reprinted by permission of the publishers and Trustees of the Loeb Classical Library from Aelian: *On the Characteristics of Animals*, Loeb Classical Library Vol. I, Books 1-5, translated by A. F. Schofield, Cambridge, Mass.: Harvard University Press, 1958-1959. The Loeb Classical Library is a registered trademark of the President and Fellows of Harvard College.
'The Playing Fields of Hogwarts', *The New York Times*, 10 October 1999. Copyright © Pico Iyer. Reprinted by permission of Pico Iyer.
The Encyclopedia of Witches and Witchcraft by Rosemary Ellen Guiley (New York, Facts on File, 1999). Copyright © 1999 Rosemary Ellen Guiley, reprinted by permission of Facts on File Inc.

Every effort has been made to trace copyright holders, but in a few cases this has proved impossible. The editor and publishers would be happy to deal with any enquiries retrospectively.

Bibliography

Borges, Jorge Luis, with Margarita Guerrero. *The Book of Imaginary Beings* (New York: Dutton, 1969).

Brewer, Ebenezer Cobham. *Brewer's Dictionary of Phrase and Fable* (New York: Harper, 1952).

Campbell, Joseph. *The Hero with a Thousand Faces* (Princeton: Princeton University Press, 1968).

Clute, John, and John Grant. *The Encyclopedia of Fantasy* (New York: St. Martin's, 1999).

Culpeper, Nicholas. *Culpeper's Complete Herbal* (New York: W. Foulsham, 1923)

Culpeper, Nicholas. *The English Physician* [The English Physitian] (London: Peter Cole, 1652). Hypertext edition courtesy of Harvey Cushing/John Hay Whitney Medical Library, Yale University, New Haven.
http://info.med.yale.edu/library/historical/culpeper/culpeper.htm

Foster, Robert. *The Complete Guide to Middle-earth* (New York: Ballantine, 1979).

Guiley, Rosemary Ellen. *The Encyclopedia of Ghosts and Spirits* (New York: Facts on File, 2000).

Guiley, Rosemary Ellen. *The Encyclopedia of Witches and Witchcraft* (New York: Facts on File, 1999).

Helms, Randel. *Tolkien's World* (Boston: Houghton Mifflin, 1974).

Le Guin, Ursula K. *A Wizard of Earthsea* (Berkeley, California: Parnassus Press, 1968).

Lepper, John Heron. *Famous Secret Societies* (London: Sampson Low, Marston & Co. Ltd, 1932).

Nigg, Joseph. *The Book of Fabulous Beasts: A Treasury of Writings from Ancient Times to the Present* (New York: Oxford University Press, 1999).

Nigg, Joseph. *Wonder Beasts: Tales and Lore of the Phoenix, the Griffin, the Unicorn and the Dragon* (Englewood, CO: Libraries Unlimited, 1995).

South, Malcolm. *Mythical and Fabulous Creatures: a Source Book and Research Guide* (New York: Greenwood, 1987).

Ogden, Tom. *Wizards and Sorcerers: from Abracadabra to Zoroaster* (New York: Facts on File: 1977).

Rose, Carol. *Giants, Monsters, and Dragons: An Encyclopedia of Folklore, Legend, and Myth* (Santa Barbara, California: ABC-CLIO, 2000).

Rose, Carol. *Spirits, Fairies, Leprechauns, and Goblins: An Encyclopedia* (New York: Norton, 1998).

Tolkien, J. R. R. *The Lord of the Rings* (Boston: Houghton Mifflin, 1965).

White, T. H. *The Sword in the Stone* (New York: Putnam's, 1939).

Willis, Roy. *Dictionary of World Myth* (London: Duncan Baird, 1995).

Van Den Broek, R., *The Myth of the Phoenix* (Leiden: E.J. Brill, 1972).

Internet resources of interest:

Steve Vander Ark's 'Harry Potter Lexicon':
http://www.i2k.com/~svderark/lexicon

The Leaky Cauldron:
http://www.the-leaky-cauldron.org/

Mike Gray's 'Quick Quotes' archives of Rowling articles and interviews:
http://www.the-leaky-cauldron.org/quickquotes/index.html

'The Magical Worlds of Harry Potter':
http://www.magicalpotter.com

Notes

In most cases, reference is made in the text to the original source. For classic texts such as *The Odyssey*, interested readers will find many excellent translations and editions. Here is further information:

Introduction
page 16: Online chat with J. K. Rowling at Barnes & Noble.com (www.bn.com), 20 October, 2000.
page 16: 'it's the sort of touch': 'Wild About Harry', TIME, 20 September 1999, Paul Gray, Elizabeth Gleick, Andrea Sachs.
page 16: J. R. R. Tolkien's essay 'On Fairy-Stories' (1938), quoted in Helms, Randel, *Tolkien's World* (Boston: Houghton, 1974).

Animagus
page 28: Online chat with J. K. Rowling at America Online, 19 October 2000.
page 29: 'Rowling says Harry will not become an Animagus': Speech at National Press Club, Washington, D.C., 20 October 2000.

Basilisks
page 34: 'He kills all trees and shrubs': Pliny the Elder [C. Plinius Secundus], *The Historie of the World*, translated by Philemon Holland, Book VIII (1601).

Beasts
page 36: 'Winds howl': Pliny the Elder [C. Plinius Secundus], *The Historie of the World*, translated by Philemon Holland, Book VIII (1601).
page 37: 'When the fish of the sea': Translated by James Carlill and included in *The Epic of the Beast*, ed. by William Rose (1900).
page 37: 'the fact that certain animals': Aristotle, *Historium Animalium*, translated by D'Arcy Wentworth Thompson. From *The Works of Aristotle*, vol. 4 (Oxford: Clarendon Press, 1910). Quoted in Nigg.
page 38: 'lives in the midst of flame': Isidore of Seville,, *An Encyclopedia of the Dark Ages*, trans. by Ernest Brehaut (New York, 1912). Quoted in Nigg.

page 38: 'Oh, come though dear infant': Goethe, Johann Wolfgang von, *The Poems of Goethe*, trans. by E.A. Bowring (New York: T.Y. Crowell & Co., 1882).

Black, Sirius

page 42: 'Magical creature expert': Rose, Carol, *Spirits, Fairies, Leprechauns, and Goblins: An Encyclopedia* (New York: Norton, 1998) page 42.

page 42: where the souls of humans travelled: Temple, Robert K. G., *The Sirius Mystery* (Rochester: Destiny Books, 1976).

page 43: guide one's soul: Lamy, Lucie, *Egyptian Mysteries* (New York: Crossroad, 1981).

page: 45: quotations regarding black dogs: G. MacEwan, *Mystery Animals of Britain and Ireland* (London: Robert Hale, 1968); Bord, J. and Bord, C., *Alien Animals* (London: Panther Books, 1985). Cited at web site of Simon Sherwood, Ph.D. candidate, University of Edinburgh Department of Psychology: http://moebius.psy.ed.ac.uk/~simon/homepage/blackdog.htm

Broomsticks

page 49: Holmes: from *The Broomstick Train*, 1891.

Cauldrons

page 53: Francis Potter: See letter quoted in Jardine, Lisa, *On a Grander Scale* (New York: HarperCollins, 2002) page 88.

Dark Mark

page 59: 'the Devil makes a mark on them': Sinistrari, Ludovico Maria, *Demoniality*, translated by the Rev. Montague Summers (London, The Fortune Press, 1927).

Death Eaters

page 61: 'Rowling says the Death Eaters were originally known as': 'Newsnight', British Broadcasting Corporation, 19 December, 2003.

Dragons

page 71: J. R. R. Tolkien's essay 'On Fairy-Stories' (1938), quoted in Helms, Randel, *Tolkien's World* (Boston: Houghton, 1974).

page 71: 'To kill a dragon': Clute, John, and John Grant, *The Encyclopedia of Fantasy* (New York: St. Martin's, 1999).

page 72: 'The dragon is the largest of all serpents': from Isidore of Seville, *An Encyclopedist of the Dark Ages*. Translated by Ernest Brehaut (New York 1912), quoted in Nigg, Joseph, *The Book of Fabulous Beasts* (New York: Oxford, 1999).

page 73: 'dreadful fore-warnings': *Anglo-Saxon Chronicle*. Translated by Rev. James Ingram (London: Longman, Hurst, 1823). Amendments by the author of this volume.

page 75: 'There is cut out of the dragon's brain': Solinus, From *The worthie work of Iulius Solinus Polyhistor contayning many noble actions of humaine creatures . . . translated out of Latin into English by Arthur Golding, Gent.* (Facsimile of 1587 edition. Gainesville, FL: Scholars' Facsimiles & Reprints, 1955).

Druids

page 77: 'discuss and teach to the youth': *Caesar's Commentaries on the Gallic and Civil Wars: with the Supplementary Books attributed to Hirtius; Including the Alexandrian, African and Spanish Wars*, 6.14. Translated by W. A. McDevitte and W. S. Bohn. Harper & Brothers, New York, 1869.

Egypt

page 89: 'He who is a priest': quoted by Michael Poe, www.sibyllinewicca.org/ lib_historical/ lib_h_egypt4.htm

Fawkes

page 91: 'There is a bird': More, Brookes. *Ovid's Metamorphoses in English blank verse* (Boston: The Cornhill Publishing Company, 1933)

page 92: 'I am the keeper': *The Book of the Dead*; an English translation, by E. A. Wallis Budge (London, K. Paul, Trench, Trübner, 1901).

Flamel

page 95: 'Flamel, look at this book': Flamel, Nicolas, *Nicolas Flamel, his explanation of the hieroglyphicall figures,* etc., by Eirenaeus Orandus (London, 1624)

page 96: 'finally I found': Flamel, Nicholas, *Testament of Nicolas Flamel*, quoted in Askin, Wade, *The Sorcerer's Handbook* (New York: Philosophical Library, 1974).

Fortescue

page 104: 'My ideal writing space': originally in *The High*, the magazine of Edinburgh's Broughton High School, from interview conducted by students Nicola Nairn, Adam Knight, and Jennifer Milne. Quoted here from 'J. K. Rowling's Fame Spoils Her Café Culture', Brian Ferguson, *Edinburgh Evening News*, 6 February 2003.

Giants

page 107: 'If you want to grace the burial place': Geoffrey of Monmouth, *History of the Kings of Britain*, translated by Sebastian Evans (New York: Dutton 1920).

Giant Squid

page 110: 'Before my eyes was a horrible monster': *Twenty Thousand Leagues Under the Sea*, from The Omnibus Verne (J. B. Lippincott Company, Garden City, NY, 1873).

Goblins

page 116: 'They hated all things': Foster, Robert, *The Complete Guide to Middle-earth* (New York: Ballantine, 1978) p. 388.

Griffins

page 119: 'I have heard': Aelian, *On Animals*, quoted in Nigg.

page 121: 'A fabulous animal': Biedermann, Hans, *Dictionary of Symbolism* (Meridian, 1994).

page 122: 'The griffin is very popular': Franklyn, Julian, Shield and Crest (New York: Sterling, 1961).

Herbology
page 126: 'I used to collect': '60 Minutes', CBS News, New York, 12 September 1999.

Hippogriff
page 132: 'They descended from the mountain': Bulfinch, Thomas, *The Age of Fable: or Beauties of Mythology*, Rev. Ed (New York: Review of Reviews company, 1913).
page 134: 'Hawk and eagle soar': *The Orlando Furioso*, translated into English verse by William Stewart Rose (London, Bell, 1907-10).

Hogwarts
page 135: 'Here are all the rites': from 'The Playing Fields of Hogwarts', Pico Iyer, *The New York Times*, 10 October 1999.
page 135: 'Hogwarts is located in Scotland': Online chat with J. K. Rowling at Barnes & Noble.com (www.bn.com), 8 September 1999.

Latin
page 142: Online chat with J. K. Rowling at Barnes & Noble.com (www.bn.com), 20 October 2000.

Manticore
page 149: 'There is in India': Aelian, *On Animals*, quoted in Nigg.
page 152: 'The gleam of my scarlet hair': Gustave Flaubert, *The Temptation of St. Anthony*, translated by Lafcadio Hearn (New York, Grosset and Dunlap, 1932).

Merpeople
page 158: 'I fancied you': Hawthorne, Nathaniel, 'The Village Uncle', in *Twice-Told Tales* (Boston: Ticknor, 1849).

Mirrors
page 160: 'Buy a looking glass': *The Encyclopedia of Witches and Witchcraft* (New York: Facts on File, 1999).

Names
page 165: 'Rowling says Harry': J. K. Rowling on 'The Connection, National Public Radio, 12 October 1999; several other names: Barnes & Noble Online, 19 March 1999.
page 166: 'Rowling says Ron Weasley': 'Harry Potter and Me', British Broadcasting Corporation, BBC1, 28 December 2001.
page 183: thestrals: Royal Albert Hall interview, 26 June 2003.

Order of the Phoenix
page 190: 'For the right moment': quoted in Cole, Margaret, *The Story of Fabian Socialism* (Stanford, CA: Stanford University Press, 1961).

Potter, Harry

page 207: 'A sudden quarrel broke out': *Histories of the Kings of Britain*, translated by Sebastian Evans (New York: Dutton, 1920).

Trolls

page 230: 'I'll come to your bedside at midnight tonight': *Peer Gynt*, translated by R. Farquharson Sharp (London, J. M. Dent; New York, E.P. Dutton, 1921).

Unicorns

page 240: 'a most swift beast': Pliny the Elder [C. Plinius Secundus], *The Historie of the World*, translated by Philemon Holland, Book VIII (1601).

page 240: 'The elder is formed': *The Travels of Ludovico de Varthenta in Egypt, Arabia Deserta and Arabia Felix, in Persia, India, and Ethiopia*, AD 1503–1508, trans. John Winter Jones, ed. George Percy Badger (London: Hakluyt Society, 1863), quoted in Nigg.

page 241: 'never become tamed': Pliny, as page 180.

page 241: 'Time's glory': Shakespeare, *The Rape of Lucrece*.

page 243: 'There are in India certain wild asses': Ctesias, *Indica*. From *Ancient India as Described by Ktesias the Knidian*, ed. J. W. McCrindle, 1882.

Veela

page 245: 'Two brothers': adapted from *Hero Tales and Legends of the Serbians* by Vojislav Petrovic (London: G. G. Harrap & Company, 1914).

Voldemort

page 249: 'A Dark Lord has often been': see entry for 'Dark Lord' in Clute, John, *The Encyclopedia of Fantasy* (New York: St. Martin's, 1999) p. 250.

page 250: 'racist': TIME, 30 October 2000.

page 250: 'takes what he perceives': transcript of 'Hot Type with Evan Solomon', Canadian Broadcasting Corporation, original broadcast 23 June 2000.

Wizards

page 255: 'psychically sensitive': Guiley, Rosemary Ellen, *The Encyclopedia of Ghosts and Spirits* (New York: Checkmark Books, Facts on File, 2000) page 383.

page 262: 'When they reached': *The Odyssey of Homer done into English Prose*. S. H. Butcher and A. Lang (London: Macmillan, 1879).

All illustrations come from the Dover Publication art collection and ArtToday.com except for: pages 50 and 258 (reproduced with slight alteration from Ogden, Tom, *Wizards and Sorcerers: from Abracadabra to Zoroaster*. New York: Facts on File: 1997); and page 169, courtesy of the Cruikshank Collection of Drawings and Prints, Princeton University.

Index

About the Author

Formerly an editorial director of HarperCollins and a head writer of television's *Who Wants To Be a Millionaire?*, David Colbert is also the author of *The Magical Worlds of The Lord of the Rings* and the *Eyewitness* history series. A graduate of Brown University, he studied anthropology and mythology but spent most of his time reading randomly in the library. He still does little else.

He can be reached at MagicalWorlds@aol.com. For news and updates, or information about requesting permission to quote from this book, visit www.magicalpotter.com.

Also Available from Puffin

THE MAGICAL WORLDS OF
THE LORD OF THE RINGS
by David Colbert

'Colbert tells the fascinating stories behind Tolkien and his masterpiece in a format accessible to adults and children alike. This is a treasure chest . . . that will enhance every reader's enjoyment of a great classic.' – *Good Book Guide*

THE MAGICAL WORLDS OF
HARRY POTTER
Spellbinding Map and Book of Secrets
by David Colbert

This stunning visual companion contains a magnificent poster-sized map, showing the mythical creatures, legendary characters, historical figures and real places woven into the *Harry Potter* stories. The accompanying Book of Secrets reveals more facts behind these magical places and people. Both are beautifully illustrated in full colour by artist Virginia Allyn.